28 DAYS OF POSITIVITY

28 DAYS OF POSITIVITY

*How to crush negativity
and release a lifetime of greatness
in less than a month*

Zeena Hicks

Sansoms Books

The Art of Perception Ltd. trading as Sansoms Books
124 City Road, London EC1V 2NX, England

www.sansomsbooks.com

For my husband and our two beautiful boys,
who are a constant reminder
of the benefits of staying positive.

Thank you for inspiring me to be a happier me!

CONTENTS

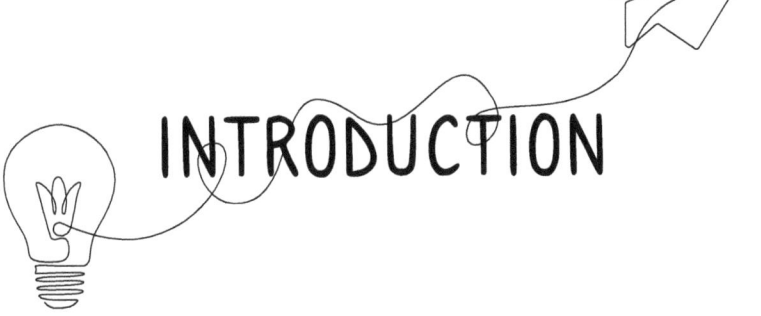

Are you surviving or are you thriving?

What would it look like if you could live and be your happiest self? Would you be where you are now, spending your time with the same people, doing the same things you are doing day in and day out? If you have ever pondered these questions and feel like you are a little bit stuck or not moving forward quickly enough, then this book may contain just what you need to get unstuck and reset your trajectory using simplified concepts, tools, and practices from, and inspired by, the field of positive psychology.

If you are new to positive psychology or are not quite sure what it is, you may be surprised to see some familiar processes as you move through the next 28 days. Don't be confused with positive psychology as an unwavering commitment to maintaining a positive state 24/7. While there is an element of embracing positive, happy thoughts and trying to maintain a positive outlook on life, the practice of positive psychology aims to make physiological, sustainable changes that permeate through many different aspects of your life, including your health and wellbeing, your relationships, and your future prospects.

Recognizing how you perceive positivity within yourself and in others, would be a useful starting point. It may be that you know a person who lives staunchly "positive". All that they touch or do has a warm and fuzzy approach. Everything is wonderful, and life is just awesome, even when their world appears to be crashing around them. If it is raining, they state how wonderful this is for nature and all living things; if they are ill, they embrace the opportunity to engage in self-healing without a pill in sight; or when they have experienced a traumatic breakup, they announce that the universe has their back, and the right person is on the way to them! Living "positively" can appear to some as being a bit saccharine sweet, a smidge woo-woo, and perhaps a little bit fake. But does it actually work? And, is there a difference between "having a positive outlook" or being a "glass half full" kind of person and practicing positive psychology?

Christopher Peterson, one of the founders of positive psychology, says that "positive psychology is the scientific study of what makes life most worth living."[1] This statement validates that positivity does have a large body of research behind it and therefore has some proven methods to help turn your life around. To put it generally, it focuses on the positive aspects of life to potentially counteract all the bad stuff we have to deal with on a daily basis. Before positive psychology, most of the studies conducted on human emotions and mental health focused on what was wrong with a person rather than what was right.

So, will positive psychology make you into a starry-eyed preacher of joy, happiness, and unconditional love? Who knows!? It may very much depend on your starting point, your commitment to the process, and your intent. What it will do, though, is help you think differently. It will enable you to instill extra positive habits, so you are more aware of when negativity and bad energy creep in to bring you down long before it gets hold of you. Be aware, that on the outside, those who live with a positive psychology mindset may look just like anyone else. They may not necessarily smile any more or less than others, but what they have is an inner confidence that radiates throughout their life that enables good things to happen and shapes their life for the better, so they are much more likely to get what they want in life.

This book was written to give you, the reader, a simple, accessible, and hopefully easily digestible way for you to tap into what is known as "The Good Life". Whether you wish to improve or protect your mental health, acquire more knowledge to help others, or get into the right energy field to manifest your heart's desire, each chapter will guide you towards a recipe, formula or simple "HOW" to be one's best self! Unlike lots of specific wellbeing practices, positive psychology offers lots of choices to figure out what works for you as an individual and to discover an abundant toolkit to help you bypass the natural negative bias that everyone has lurking beneath as human beings.

Each person's natural negative bias has a great purpose. In basic terms, it keeps you safe. It is always on the lookout for danger. It is what has kept humans alive for 300,000 years or more. Homo sapiens (translated as "wise human" from Latin) have overcome a huge number of obstacles to be the dominant species on this earth, but at what cost?

Despite all the evolution, our minds could be perceived as somewhat limited. Yes, sure, we are discovering many more ways to "fix" things, like some diseases, global warming, and poverty, but what if instead of 'fixing' things, we were able to stop these negative impacts from occurring? Kind of like pressing the rewind button. Imagine a world and society where we didn't have pandemics, inequality and global warming, or fight wars with wars; where nature and people were given a chance to heal? It all started and can end with the human race. By starting with ourselves, we might just be able to take the first steps towards this seemingly unimaginable future. The influence we have not only on ourselves, but on the wider world, could be boundless, if we choose to broaden our lens.

Many of us live in a teeny tiny bubble that shows us what we wish to see every day. This narrow lens is influenced by our past experiences, our culture, our upbringing, our family and peers, our education, etc. Our brain amazingly filters out much of the information that is not in our line of focus, and it will tend to look for things that reinforce the way we think and feel. The reticular activating system (RAS) in the brain is partially responsible for this. In a similar way that social media or search engines filter out what they feel is most relevant for you based on your interests, the RAS filters down the information it thinks that you want to receive.

If you were to see and hear everything that was in front of you every moment of every day, your brain would literally explode (okay, I haven't got that fact-checked, but it seems quite plausible, and you get my gist)! The RAS uses a large portion of your subconscious downloads as a guide to try and ensure that you are not exposed to anything that could potentially harm you (this does not always work, but we will get on to that later!). Therefore, depending on your "personal lens," you will generally see what is aligned with your personal values, wants, goals, and points of expectation from past experiences. As a result, you will be pretty much living unconsciously.

Whilst, for the most part, your personal lens filters out and prevents you from seeing and hearing what you do not want to see, it equally presents to you what you are looking for, even subconsciously. In simple terms, if you are programmed to notice negativity, you will find it quite easily, in people, in circumstances, in the media, and in your experiences. Luckily, the same can be said for positivity. If you are tuned in, living, and feeling positive, you will start to see things differently and discover great things lurking around every corner. You will notice things to be grateful for, and life will hand you roses.

Now, if you have had a wonderful, carefree life full of sunflowers, unicorns, and rainbows, then you might be all good, and this book may simply provide validation that life is good. However, if, like most people, you have had some difficult challenges, unsavory experiences, and current or previous relationship conflicts in your life, then your subconscious program might need some attention. Taking the opportunity to gain back some control and reprogram your RAS[2] by becoming more intentional will be hugely beneficial for you. I, therefore, applaud you for picking up this book and taking those first steps to bypass your subconscious negativity bias and find out why life is worth living!

Take some time before you start to download the accompanying pdf workbook, which will support your learning, on: www.zeenahicks.com/28days-positivity

How to use this book

In an ideal world, you would set aside 28 consecutive days to commit to, discover, and explore a new state of being. Knowing, however, what life is like, the structure of the book enables you to pick up from where you left off at any time and continue on your quest to live more positively. You may feel like dipping in and out of the book or skipping over parts that don't really resonate, which is also fine too. This is your journey, and finding what works for you will be a crucial part of embedding these processes and creating more positive habits in your life. The only thing I might suggest is that if something feels uncomfortable at first, take a breath and persevere, as this may be the very activity that holds the biggest growth potential. When you feel uncomfortable, it often means that your body and mind are trying to protect you from something. That something, however, might be what you need to move from your normal state.

At the end of each day, you will be encouraged to reflect on the activity you have recently completed. Use the questions, guidance and suggestions offered in the reflection section and jot down your answers in the notes spaces provided at the end of each day to explore a little deeper and make new discoveries. You will also be offered the choice to extend that day's activity for longer as you move through the other days for increased impact. Remember, positive repetition is your friend, and this will help you start to form new positive habits.

What you will need

Apart from having an open mind, it would be advisable to get yourself a special notebook to write down your reflections, thoughts, plans, and actions throughout your 28-day journey, although I have included lots of spaces throughout this book to write. If you do choose to use a special notebook, look out for a journal style book that is a little bit different and worth keeping. You can continue to add your reflections long after you have completed this book, and hopefully, it will be something that you will keep over the years to see how far you have come.

I have included a shout-out to some of my personal favorite books at the end of each day if you wish to dive deeper into any of the topics which resonate most with you. At the time of writing, I have no relationship or affiliation with any of these authors or books, but I feel that a good book is worth shouting about and they are among my personal favorites. You may, however, choose to wait until the end of the 28 days before delving into the many other awesome books which can help you further learn, develop, and grow ;-)

Your intentions

As mentioned earlier in the introduction, when you focus on what you want rather than what you don't want in life, your reticular activating system (RAC) finds a way of showing it to you. With that in mind, write a few notes to define what it is you intend to achieve by the end of these 28 days. It might be a physical thing, an achievement, a specific feeling or emotion, or a better relationship with someone. Try and formulate crystal-clear objectives by answering the following questions and writing them down:

What do I want to achieve by the end of these 28 days of Positivity?

How do I intend to get there - what actions will I choose to take?

Why is this important to me?

How can I measure my success - how will I know that I have gotten there?

What is the consequence of my not achieving this objective?

At the end of each chapter, you will find space to collate your findings. Use this section to take notes on any discoveries that you make each day or collectively at the end of each week. Alternatively, you may wish to add them to your notebook or journal, including your thoughts and realizations as you move through the next 28 days. Remember, this is your journey; trust the path you choose will be the right one for you at this time.

WEEK ONE - ME, MYSELF, AND I

Over the next four weeks, you will discover 28 positive psychology-inspired tools and practices to help you disrupt any underlying negative patterns you might be subconsciously (or consciously) hiding, so you can start looking for the positive things in life.

In Week One of 28 Days of Positivity, you will be introduced to a number of ways to help heighten your awareness of self. Building this self-awareness is perhaps one of the most important things you can do for your own mental health, wellbeing, and life satisfaction, as it is the first fundamental step in helping you understand more of who you are and what makes you tick. Being self-aware enables you to look at yourself objectively, with better clarity over your thoughts, recognizing the influence of your thoughts and emotions on your own behaviors and how others perceive you.

If you feel you are already pretty self-aware, I challenge you to look again this week and throw yourself into the process of self-discovery. This week will challenge you to look deeper and, whether you resonate or not with what you experience or see, try to approach each day with an open mind without judging yourself or the process along the way.

The more you look for it, the more you may realize that everyone has big chunks of the day when lack of awareness can be observed. For example, have you ever felt a little bit sad, and you don't know why; or maybe you were in a conversation with someone, and you responded in a tone that was "unlike you"; or you did something that was perceived by another in a way you never intended? If you recognize yourself in any of these situations, you will have experienced your unconscious programming at work.

Throughout week one, you will go back to basics and uncover what is lurking within you. You will start to understand the lens through which you view your world a little bit better, discover a few (or many) unconscious biases, and tap into what makes you the best you.

Your objective in this initial week is to just observe and learn with curiosity and without expectation. As mentioned before, your mission is not to judge yourself or the process. At this point, you are not trying to change anything. Just allow yourself to be, which basically means stop getting in the way of you being your true beautiful self!

As with everything contained in this book, the emphasis is on exploration and discovery, so just have fun with it ;-)

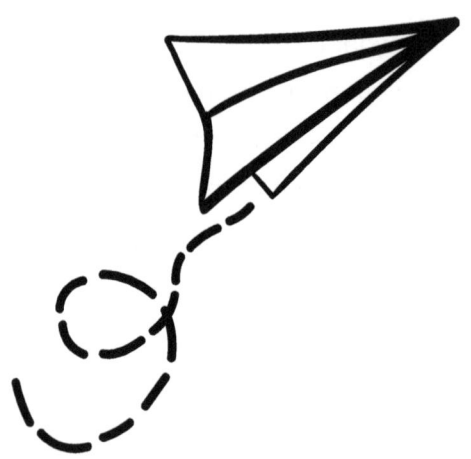

Your Thoughts

*"To become different from what
we are, we must have some
awareness of what we are."*

– ERIC HOFFER

Your Thoughts

How aware are you? On day one, you will focus your attention on your mind and what goes on there. Your mind plays a huge part in your behavioral patterns. The thoughts you have throughout the day can have a huge impact on how you feel and what you do. Your thoughts can inspire you, encourage you, and liberate you, but they can also keep you stuck. Research suggests that the average person has around 6,000 "thought worms,"[3] or streams of thought topics each day. Sounds like a lot, eh? If ever there was proof that you live your life mostly unaware, then this is it! It is quite plausible that if you engaged in every thought you had, you likely would not make it through the day. What the exercise today will do is to identify just a small portion of your thinking that might be keeping you limited.

The first activity will be simply to become aware of when any negative, judgmental, or unwanted thoughts crop up. It could be that during your day you find yourself thinking, "I'm not good enough", "I can't do this", or "It's not possible". It could be an unfounded judgment of others or of a situation, such as "I really don't want to speak to this person", or "This is difficult", or even suggesting, "This is really bad". It might otherwise be that you are experiencing a mood that has been going on for a day, a couple of days, or even a couple of weeks, where you've been feeling a bit down, but you don't know why, and you can't seem to get clarity of your thoughts. Each of these scenarios may be your negativity bias controlling your thoughts.

So today, in this inaugural task, without judging yourself, just notice any negative, judgmental, or unwanted thoughts that arise for you. The most important part of this exercise is just becoming aware without analyzing yourself or the thoughts you are thinking! For example, when you notice several negative things popping up in a row, avoid the temptation to berate yourself for being so negative. Or, it may be that you keep forgetting to notice, and you conclude that this is "hopeless" or "not for you!" Stick with it no matter what comes up for you. This is simply an awareness exercise.

The great thing is that once you become aware, you can start to divert negative thoughts before these "thought worms" become emotionally connected, driving negative behaviors or, at worst, full-blown catastrophizing. The first step is to notice and become aware of your patterns of thought. To reiterate, on this day, the purpose is nothing more than to increase awareness. You may wish to carry out this exercise beyond the first day and throughout the first week to give you better insight and to support the rest of the awareness-building work, but this is your journey to choosing what works for you.

Later, as you get more confident and more consciously aware, you can start to use this technique to influence the behavior of others towards you, but more on that later. And please don't worry if you find your day is one big negative stream. Celebrate the fact that you are noticing and keep curious. Remember, as mentioned previously, it is not about dwelling on the negative; it is simply just to notice.

Becoming self-aware is the fundamental step in any health and wellbeing program. Try and be patient with yourself, as you may not gain your awareness superpower in just one day, but it won't be long before you notice those moody mind moments and disrupt the pattern and start to change. Soon you will become more conscious and gain more control over how you think, feel, and behave. In time, you will be able to use this superpower to influence how others behave around you! But, today, on day one, just be aware…

TASK 1

Wear a band, bracelet, elastic, or scrunchie on your wrist for the day—something that doesn't stop your blood flow!

Look out for any judgments or negative thoughts or patterns that come to mind today. When you notice something arising for you, don't try to analyze, change, or engage with the discovery. Simply switch the band from one wrist to the other and continue doing this throughout the day.

You may want to write down what is causing you to move your band each time and see if there are any patterns in your thoughts, feelings, or behaviors at the end of the day.

For an insightful read, check out: Insight: The Power of Self-Awareness in a Self-Deluded World *by Tasha Eurich* ☺

Judgment Spotting - Reflection

On day one, you explored and monitored your thoughts and judgments. You may wish to write down what you discover. Did you find the exercise easy or challenging? Were you able to catch all those thoughts and judgments as they occurred? Did you find that the band constantly moved throughout the day, or did you find yourself forgetting about it, and it remained static until you got annoyed with yourself and gave up? There is no right or wrong way for this exercise to go.

If you discovered that the band constantly moved throughout the day and found yourself full of thoughts and judgments, well done! You may have come to some realization that the mind is in a constant flow of activity with or without your awareness.

If you found the band didn't move much, well done! It may be that your focus was on other things throughout the day and that awareness of your inner thoughts and judgments is not currently at the forefront of your mind. This is a great realization and discovery and is perfect for where you are right now.

Next steps

You have two options:

1. You may wish to keep the band on your wrist for the rest of the week as you carry out the weekly activities to further build awareness of your subconscious thoughts and judgments.

2. Write a few observational notes on what you discovered and move on to Day 2 with a new focus.

Whatever you decide, it is your journey towards self-awareness!

TAKE NOTE

Your Breath

"Breath is the bridge which connects life to consciousness, which unites your body to your thoughts."

– THICH NHAT HANH

Your Breath

Are you breathing properly? To continue building awareness of self, day two aims to help you connect more consciously with your breath. The exercise today will explore the most optimum way of breathing, which may prove beneficial to both your health and wellbeing.

When you were born, your body knew exactly what to do as you took that first breath. From birth through to death, you will continue a cycle of inhaling oxygen and exhaling carbon dioxide, mostly without ever really thinking about it. Most people rarely, if ever, question whether the air will be available for them to breathe and trust that their body knows what to do to stay alive.

If you watch a young baby breathe while they sleep, you may notice that their abdomen rises and falls in a slow rhythmic movement, silently and peacefully. Breathing happens solely through the nose up until six months of age. As the infant grows through childhood and adolescence, experiencing both the beauty and the sometimes unpleasant, breathing patterns change, most often without the awareness of the participant. By the time a person reaches their teens, many simply forget how to breathe. If you ask a regular adult (who doesn't do any breath work) to take a deep breath, you might observe that their shoulders go up, their chest goes out, and sometimes you may even notice their abdomen going in. All of these actions are counterintuitive to healthy breathing.

It is estimated that almost half of people breathe through their mouths, and this can be quite common in the morning.[4] Breathing through the nose, however, is the more natural approach for the body, and it has many more benefits for you. By simply changing your breathing through your nose rather than your mouth, you have access to 20% more oxygen. The nose also filters out many nasties and regulates the temperature of the air, essentially conditioning each intake of air. But that is not all. Research has shown that taking time out to consciously focus on your breath on a daily basis can improve your sleep, manage stress and anxiety, and even strengthen your immune system.[5]

Having a good rhythmic breathing cycle is vitally important for your wellbeing. Did you know that your natural instinct is to hold your breath when you are stressed? So, if you are noticeably stressed, and you start feeling a little lightheaded, it is very likely that you have stopped breathing! By checking in on your breath regularly and using breathing tools and techniques, you have the power to increase your energy, get clarity of focus, and lower your blood pressure and heart rate. Seems like a no-brainer, eh?!

Before you start today's exercise, it would be useful to note where your starting point is. Take a moment to observe the natural rhythm of your breath. Then, after a few regular breaths, take a slow deep breath. Watch what happens in your body. Do you tense up? Where do you feel your breath go? Your chest? Your back? Your abdomen? Did you breathe in and out through your nose or your mouth? You may wish to write down what you discover.

For the purpose of today's exercise, you are going to practice belly breathing (also known as diaphragmatic breathing or abdominal breathing). Find a comfortable position to do the exercise, either sitting with your back straight or standing tall. With one hand on your abdomen and the other on your chest, breathe in deeply through your nose. Imagine the air going through your nose, past your lungs, and deep into your abdomen. You may find visualizing a balloon being inflated and deflated as you breathe in and out useful. How big can you get this balloon to expand? The aim is to breathe deep down, expanding the abdomen and ribs while keeping the chest nice and still.

TASK 2

Today's task centers around box breathing, or square breathing.

Get yourself into a comfortable upright position and gently breathe in through your nose, deep down into the abdomen for four counts: 1, 2, 3, 4, then hold your breath for four other counts: 1, 2, 3, 4.

Breathe out through your nose for four counts: 1, 2, 3, 4, and finally, hold your breath once completely exhaled again for another four counts: 1, 2, 3, 4.

Continue this cycle for a couple of minutes to help reset and regulate your breathing.

For a breathtaking read, check out: Breath: The New Science of a Lost Art *by James Nestor* 🙂

Box Breathing - Reflection

Taking time to reflect on each activity you complete in this book will help you introduce a pause before you move on, increase your self-awareness, and help you find more meaning in the process.[6] You can hold on to those things that most resonate and let go of what you need to, allowing you to move on. Box breathing has the capacity to serve as a stress reducer in action, but in the longer term, it can help with depression and regulate the autonomic nervous system (ANS).[7]

Did you discover anything new or surprising about the way you breathe? Did you feel in any way dizzy during or after square breathing, which can be common due to the increased intake of oxygen?

Some people become more conscious of their breathing following this exercise. Like with anything new, breathing differently may feel uncomfortable, to begin with, but the more you practice, the more you and your body will get used to it. Shallow breathing into the chest can develop into an unhelpful habit, so the more you develop your awareness of how you breathe and allow your breath to travel from your nose deep into your abdominal area, the better this will be for your health.

Next steps

You have two options:

1. Set yourself some time every day to do a three-minute breathing exercise. Use your phone to set an alarm two or three times throughout the day to stop, check in with your breathing, and practice the box breathing technique.

2. Write a few observational notes on what you discovered and move on to Day 3 with a new focus.

Whatever you decide, it is your journey towards building your self-awareness.

TAKE NOTE !!!

DAY 3

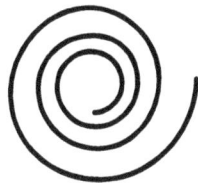

Your Emotions

"Thoughts create emotions, emotions create feelings, and feelings create behavior. So, it's very important that our thoughts are positive to attract the right people, events, and circumstances into our lives."

– AVIS J. WILLIAMS

Your Emotions

How would you like to feel every day? On day one, you spent time noticing your thoughts and naturally occurring judgments. Today aims to expand your awareness even further by delving into the depths of your mind to further try and bypass your automation process. From what we know in psychology, every human is hard-wired to think, feel, and react unconsciously. This is both incredibly useful but also downright unhelpful at times. Day one focused on catching those negative thought worms, but day three explores the impact of these thoughts on your feelings and emotions.

One of the foundational principles in psychological therapies, such as Cognitive Behavioral Therapy (CBT)[8] and Neuro-linguistic Programming (NLP)[9], is the cycle of thinking, feeling, and behaving. Depending on where you look, this process is known by a variety of different labels, including the Cognitive Triangle, Model of Emotions, Mercedes Model, Thoughts, Feelings, Behavior Cycle, etc., but ultimately it demonstrates that your behaviors, feelings, and thoughts are intrinsically linked. Therefore, if you want to make a positive change in your life, it would be valuable for you to increase your understanding of this cycle.

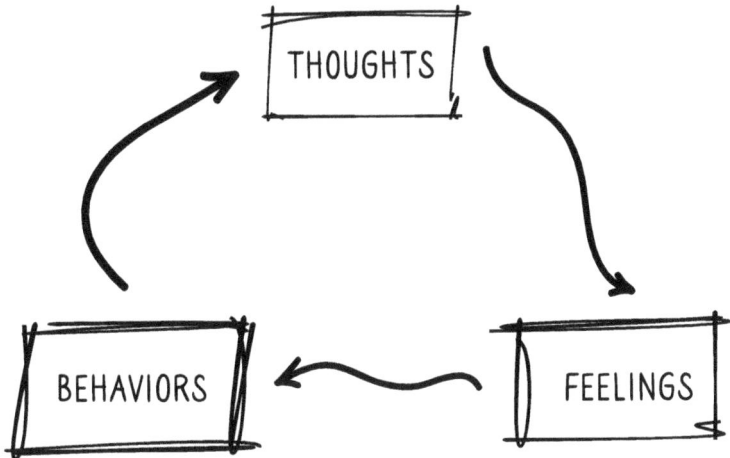

The more you become aware of your natural cycle, the more you will be able to move away from unconscious living. Of course, you may never completely stop this process, but you can start to understand any patterns you might have and introduce a pause in the cycle, giving you increased control. You can even begin to understand those around you better by observing their patterns of behavior and then start to influence their outcomes. This can become your second superpower!

Today's premise shows that for every thought you have, you will have a corresponding emotion or feeling. It can also work the other way round, so for any feeling you have, you will have a series of associated thoughts. For instance, you may see someone you are not overly fond of walking across from you, down the street. You think: "I really don't want to talk to them", and you start to feel a bit nervous that they might spot you. The feeling is instantaneously anxious, then you think of all the reasons why you don't want to talk to them. It can also happen simultaneously. What happens next, though, is key. Because you are experiencing these thoughts and feelings, your body will respond, often unconsciously, with a corresponding behavior. With its primary function to keep you safe, you might suddenly freeze, or turn swiftly, knocking into the person behind you or perhaps dive into a random shop to hide from view. This is your cognitive cycle in action. It can happen very quickly and, at times, can be incredibly subtle, like a raised eyebrow in a meeting that someone pulls you up on or a mood that has come out of nowhere. The wonderful thing is that you can disrupt the pattern and even manipulate it to work in your favor.

In today's activity, you will not only bring your awareness to this cycle of thoughts, feelings, and behaviors, but you will also work towards inducing a positive outcome. By focusing on just one area of this cognitive triangle, you can start to disrupt the cycle and evoke change. This exercise works in harmony with the activity from day one, where your focus went on catching patterns of negative thinking or judgment. Today you will look out for any corresponding emotions arising from those thoughts.

TASK 3

Today, focus on how you would like to feel. Consider a good feeling emotion to work towards all day. For example, "Today, I would like to feel healthy/happy/confident." Keep reminding yourself throughout the day how you want to feel and start to look for things that will help you achieve this feeling.

Notice any thoughts that arise as you focus on your positive feeling.

Before making any decision throughout the day, ask yourself, "Will this make me feel healthy/happy/confident?" Be led today by your emotions and feelings.

For a comprehensive read, check out: Thoughts and Feelings: Taking Control of Your Moods and Your Life *by Martha Davis, Matthew McKay, and Patrick Fanning* ☺

Feeling Positive - Reflection

The exercise on day three aimed to bring awareness to your natural cognitive cycle. What was it like to focus most of your attention on feeling good? How did it differ from your "normal day"? Did it uncover any unusual thinking patterns? Did you experience any conflict of thoughts and emotions, or were you able to just go with the flow?

If you were able to stay connected to a positive emotion for the whole or part of the day, did it have any impact on your behavior? Did anyone around you notice, or did you find the day to be different than usual? Was anybody influenced by your feelings and behavior?

Your cognitive cycle is a perpetual response that you carry with you every minute of every day. At this stage, simply observing what is happening in your mind and body and making a note of when you feel positive, negative, or neutral will be hugely beneficial for your self-awareness journey.

Next steps

You have two options:

1. Set a timer on your watch or phone to go off at random times during the day. When it pings, stop, and notice what you are thinking, feeling, and doing at the time. Make a quick note of anything that arises.

2. Write a few observational notes on what you discovered and move on to Day 4 with a new focus.

Whatever you decide, it is your journey towards building your self-awareness.

TAKE NOTE

DAY 4

Your Narrative

"It's never too late to change.
Every day is a blank page, and
your story has yet to be written."

– AMY ZHANG

Your Narrative

If you were to write the story of "you", what would it say? Each person has a very individual and unique story to tell. Sometimes this story might be freely expressed, while in others, some elements of that story are suppressed, ignored, and hidden from view. Self-stories are influenced by your family, upbringing, peer group, culture, spirituality, education, and all your past experiences, but how well is this story serving you? Today's exercise explores one small aspect of your story, focusing specifically on what you identify with as being you.

Earlier in week one, you will have started to practice becoming more self-aware. You will have explored how a great deal of your day is spent in automation, and you will hopefully have started to live a little more in the conscious, or present moment. This next step will help you identify, and begin to re-frame, the quiet little voice that you are aware of inside your head. Your inner narrative, or self-talk, is part of those 6,000 thought worms you have each day, and, as mentioned previously, its main aim is to keep you safe by cognitively processing all of the information from your past, present, and potential future.

The degree to which one's inner narrative features is very much down to each individual. Some people feel that their heads are in constant chatter, while others appear to be blissfully unaware of this dialogue. Whether or not you are aware, the dialogue is going on. It is judging people and situations, making or weighing up decisions, and, most importantly, spurring you on or bringing you down.

Understanding what this dialogue is saying in relation to who you identify as and, in particular, increasing your awareness of whether that self-talk is positive or negative is important. It is very common to catch some really unhelpful language or remarks when listening to your internal chatter, and you may find that you talk to yourself in a very different way than you might talk to a good friend. When you make a silly mistake, or you do something that you didn't mean to, what words do you say to yourself in your head? "I'm so stupid" or "You idiot" are pretty common phrases. Imagine now that your friend made the same silly mistake. Would you say the same types of words or phrases to them? Probably not!

Negative self-talk can be quite destructive, and it can, unsurprisingly, greatly affect your self-confidence, self-esteem, and mood. If someone you knew well used the same words and phrases that you use on yourself, would you accept it? If not, then why do you accept it from yourself? Unfortunately, quite often, we are not even aware of this silent abuse. Building your awareness is the first step to understanding what that narrative is. The next step is re-framing the conversation, using more positive dialogue, just as you might with a good friend. Today's activity aims to bring awareness to your inner chatter while helping you take your first footsteps towards positive re-framing, which will be covered later in the book.

Remember that the words that you speak, even if those words are just in your head, hold more power than you might think. If you find that your inner dialogue is spending lots of time "protecting you and keeping you safe" by feeding you a negative narrative, take back control, change the conversation, and choose a positive path!

Use the workbook to guide you with this next exercise on: www.zeenahicks.com/28days-positivity

TASK 4

In your notebook, draw a vertical line down the center of the page and, on the left-hand side, write down all of the things that bother, annoy, irritate, or worry you.

Now on the right-hand side, write down the opposite, in the positive—where you would rather be. For instance, "I hate getting up in the morning" now becomes "I love getting up in the mornings, bright and early".

Once you have made a list, read each positive statement out loud, separately, and slowly. Now close your eyes and listen to the narrative that comes back to you. Is it positive, negative, or neutral? Make a note and move on to the next step.

For a brilliant read, check out: Addicted to the Monkey Mind: Change the Programming That Sabotages Your Life *by J.F. Benoist* ☺

Refining Your Narrative - Reflection

Spending time in your head when it is particularly chatty can sometimes be an unpleasant experience. But the more time you spend there objectively, the more you can learn your patterns of behavior and implement change.

The process of writing those things that are challenging or conflicting with you and re-framing them enables you to start to look at situations differently. When you start to re-frame, you might notice increased opposition, arguing that "this is not real". Be aware that neuroscience shows that the brain does not know the difference between what is real and what is not. The chemical response is almost the same as what you think to what you experience, so let your imagination run wild!

In your notes, you may wish to reflect on how this exercise felt. Did you get stuck on anything specific? Did you experience any positive feelings from the activity, or did it just make the negative narrative more obvious? Perhaps you became more aware of those irritations or worries following the practice session and were able to catch and change the narrative. At this stage, just observe.

Next steps

You have two options:

1. To continue building awareness of your inner dialogue, set an alarm to go off at different times of the day each day. When it goes off, close your eyes and "check in" with your inner narrative. What are you thinking? How does it make you feel? Write in your notebook, without judgment, what is going on for you at this time.

2. Write a few observational notes on what you discovered and move on to Day 5 with a new focus.

Whatever you decide, it is your journey towards building your self-awareness.

TAKE NOTE

DAY 5

Character Strengths

"You have the power to positively influence your wellbeing by focusing on your highest character strengths."

– DR. RYAN NIEMIEC

Character Strengths

What makes you virtuous and strong? Character Strengths are one of the founding principles of positive psychology, which seeks to focus on what is right with people rather than what is wrong. Early in the study of positive psychology, researchers discovered that there are six virtues that are shared across cultures and societies. These positive core virtues enable individuals to survive and thrive and have been categorized as wisdom, courage, justice, humanity, transcendence, and temperance. From these virtues, 24-character strengths were identified to represent the positive assets each individual possesses, and they offer a way in which you can express your values as a person:[10]

- **Wisdom:** Creativity, curiosity, open-mindedness, love of learning, perspective

- **Courage**: Honesty, bravery, persistence, zest

- **Humanity:** Kindness, love, social intelligence

- **Justice:** Fairness, leadership, teamwork

- **Temperance:** Forgiveness, modesty, prudence, self-regulation

- **Transcendence:** Appreciation of beauty, gratitude, hope, humor, religiousness

Knowing your character strengths is just the first step towards becoming your best self. Using them as a guide to influence how you think, feel, and behave can help act as a buffer for mental illness when adopted as a way of being in your day-to-day life.

In today's activity, you will join over 21 million others to take a free online test with the VIA Institute on Character to identify your signature strengths, and you will use these to explore the world around you today.[11] There are so many ways you can use your character strengths once you discover them, but for the purpose of this exercise, the focus will be on your top five strengths, also known as your "signature strengths". That doesn't mean that your bottom five strengths are all doom and gloom—quite the opposite, as these are still strengths no matter how low they might appear in the pecking order.

Your top five strengths are best known as the ones that will take the least amount of energy from you to embrace. You might identify with them as being much more natural and less of a struggle to maintain, which is why the focus will be on these for today's exercise. Dr. Ryan Niemiec, Educational Director at VIA, says the three key features of a signature strength are:[12]

1. You feel this strength is **essential** to who you are as a person.

2. The strength is completely **effortless** to embody.

3. You feel **energized** using this strength. It makes you happy, uplifts you, and you find balance with it.

It might be that you identify with just one or two of your strengths as "signature." It might also be that you hadn't really thought about it until now, and actually, you can see yourself vividly in the top five strengths. Just go with whatever resonates with you the most in this exercise and enjoy playing.

The survey will take approximately 15 minutes to complete, so allow yourself plenty of time and answer instinctively as you are now and not as you aspire to be. You will need to register, but it is free and has stringent data protection protocols. You may also wish to invite close family members, such as partners, siblings, or children aged eight or over, to take the test and do the activity with you.

A list of the character strengths, and how you can use them most effectively, can be found in the workbook on: www.zeenahicks.com/28days-positivity

TASK 5

Complete the Via Character Strengths online survey on www.viacharacter.org/surveys/takesurvey. Download the free PDF report on completion.

Focusing on your signature strengths or top five character strengths, try and bring these strengths alive in your daily activities and conversations. Eat with them, take them for a walk, and use them in conversation, socially, or at work.

Live, breathe, and embrace these strengths and write down your findings in your journal.

For a virtuous read, check out: The Power of Character Strengths: Appreciate and Ignite Your Positive Personality *by Ryan M. Niemiec*

Character Strengths - Reflection

Were you surprised at your top five character strengths? Could you recognize yourself when reading the descriptions of the results? You may have found that having just one day to explore your character strengths was a little restrictive, and discovering their existence is only the beginning. Was the task challenging or eventful for you? If you managed to take notes on how you felt, look back over your notes and reflect on what was different for you. Was any individual-character strength easier to adopt than the others? Did your strengths complement each other, or did you find it difficult to adopt them in succession?

Each person's journey with their character strengths will be very different, and if you don't feel connected with them, persevere, and lean into them during times of stress or challenge. Lead with your strengths when making decisions or during times of discomfort. Tapping into your character strengths can work wonders in relationships, the work environment, or anywhere you wish to be persuasive or heard. Have fun exploring!

Next steps

You have two options:

1. You may wish to extend this exercise and choose just one character strength to play with each day of this week. Live with strength in mind. Embody it, utilize it in conversations, and make decisions with it in mind.

2. Write a few observational notes on what you discovered and move on to Day 6 with a new focus.

Whatever you decide, it is your journey towards building your self-awareness.

TAKE NOTE

DAY 6

Mindful Meditation

"Meditation is a process through which we get to know how our mind works and train our attention to remain where we place it."

– MICHAEL SMITH

Mindful Meditation

How mindful are you? If you are looking for a tool that can offer you a bit of calm in stressful moments, build better relationships, plan your day (or your life) more effectively, manifest the things you want, find some inner and outer peace, and much more, then look no further! Mindful meditation is a practice that is used across the world by people of all nationalities, cultures, and beliefs. While it is used as part of a spiritual practice in some countries, meditation in its secular form has been known as the cornerstone for influencing sustainable cognitive change. In other words, you can use meditation to increase your focus, become smarter, and even rewind the effects of an aging brain.[13, 14] Mindful meditation is also being used in medical settings to treat cardiovascular disease, anxiety, infertility, chronic pain, lower blood pressure, and enhance the body's immune system.[15]

If you currently have a meditation practice, you may already be won over, but if you have never tried it or have tried it once before and felt it wasn't for you, as part of this introduction, you are challenged to adopt it and persevere at least for two weeks. You WILL notice the difference.

There are almost one billion Google results for meditation, with tons of different meditation styles and theories. The exercise today explores mindfulness meditation, but once you feel you have the basics, do have fun exploring and discovering new ways to tap into your mind and change some of your old thinking, belief patterns, and behaviors.

Before you attempt the exercise, you may wish to mentally position this mindful meditation activity as mind training or exercise for the brain. In the same way, if you don't move your body regularly, you start to feel sluggish and unfit, and so, too, does your mind. If you don't exercise your mind regularly, you may rely on your automated thinking more and more and end up with a mind that is like a spaghetti junction—complicated, busy, and most often blocked.

The other super crucial thing to remember is that there is a misconception that meditation is about clearing your mind of all your thoughts. This is not the case and may actually be humanly impossible. What it does is help you become aware of, identify, and compartmentalize your thoughts so that they don't rule you and demand that you listen.

The common ground for most meditations is to focus on an anchor point. This could be on the breath, as with the exercise we will explore today, but it could also be on a body part, a sound, some music, a mantra, or a word. Whatever you choose to focus on, you will give this anchor your full attention in the present moment. The challenge is building up your brain stamina to notice when you are getting distracted (which might be a lot!) and be able to find your way back to the anchor point. You can think of it as a game trying to catch you out, noticing each thought that comes along to throw you off track. Welcome each thought as it arises and wallow in the greatness of knowing your anchor is waiting for you to reconnect. Think that every time you make it back to your anchor is the equivalent of your brain doing 20 mental push-ups!

Watch out for any internal dialogue that may try to sabotage your meditation journey. If your focus is a little erratic, and in the initial stages, your mind constantly tries to interrupt you with 'important' (not really!) messages, memories, or to-do lists, don't worry. Many people stop meditating because of this. Common excuses to give up include "My mind is too busy to meditate", "I find it hard to focus", "It's not the right time, I have too much going on", etc. This is completely normal and exactly the reason why you must persevere.

Repetition is key, so keep meditating even when it is challenging, and you will eventually start to become the master of your own mind. Use the guided breathing meditation on: www.zeenahicks.com/28days-positivity

TASK 6

Set a timer for 10 minutes.

Sit up with your back straight and, without collapsing, gently close your eyes.

Take three deep breaths, in through your nose and out through your mouth, before returning to your normal breathing pattern. Maintain your focus on your incoming and outgoing breath along with any sensations that may occur.

If any thoughts or feelings arise during the practice, just acknowledge them without engaging with them for too long and find your way back to focusing on your breath.

For a mindful read, check out: Mindfulness: A Practical Guide to Finding Peace in a Frantic World *by Danny Penman and Mark Williams* 😊

Meditation - Reflection

How did it feel taking 10 minutes out of your day to sit in stillness with your breath and your thoughts? Were you able to focus continuously on your breath as the air entered and left your body? Did you notice any sensations that arose? Was the air cold? How did it feel to follow the air moving through your nose and down into your lungs? What happened to your chest, your stomach, and your back? Did you naturally pause before and after each breath?

What about your thoughts? Did you find it hard to focus on your breath without a barrage of thoughts, feelings, and/or emotions arising, or was it easy to focus? Both responses offer a positive learning experience.

When did you do the exercise? Usually, the optimum time to meditate is when you are at your most relaxed and at a time that you can commit to on a daily basis. Meditating first thing in the morning before you do anything else can be beneficial as your brain is already in the "Alpha State" (halfway between sleeping and waking), and your mind may be more open to suggestions. Make sure you get out of bed before you meditate, or you may just fall back to sleep! Find what works for you and try and meditate as often as you can.

Next steps

You have two options:

1. Meditate daily in conjunction with the other activities for the next two weeks. In time, extend your meditation time to 15, 20, and, eventually, 30 minutes.

2. Write a few observational notes on what you discovered and move on to Day 7 with a new focus.

Whatever you decide, it is your journey towards building your self-awareness.

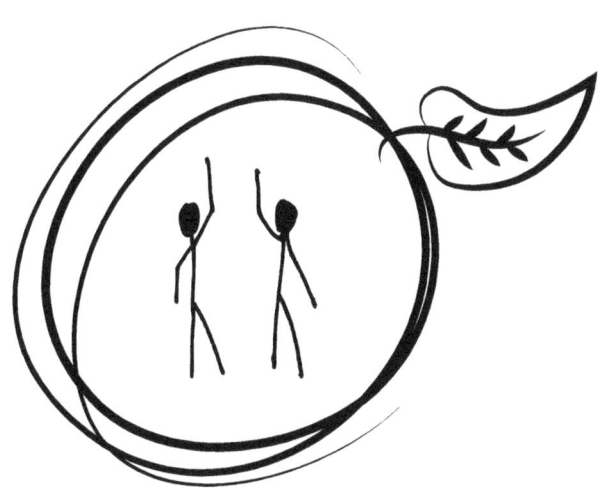

TAKE NOTE

DAY 7

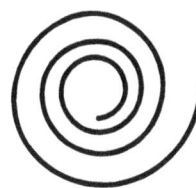

Journaling

*"A personal journal is an
ideal environment in which to
'become'. It is a perfect place
for you to think, feel, discover,
expand, remember, and dream."*

– BRAD WILCOX

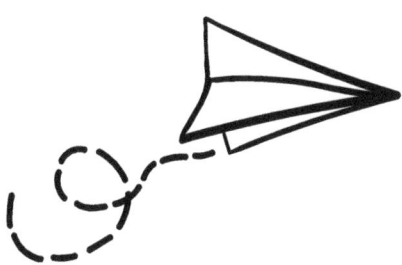

Journaling

How often do you write your thoughts down? If you completed each of the first week's activities, you might have been encouraged to write down your reflections to help with building your self-awareness. The very act of writing things down can help you work things out, express yourself, or simply offload. This is often why people find to-do lists essential, as the process of writing all the things that you have to do out of your head and on paper can create a feeling of space and clarity, increase motivation, and improve recall.[16]

Journaling as a concept has been around for centuries. Writing down ideas, thoughts, and feelings has been an activity shared by people across the globe from all walks of life. From Leonardo da Vinci, Ludwig van Beethoven, and Charles Darwin to Anne Frank, Nelson Mandela, and Oprah Winfrey. One common theme shared in some of the most famous diaries and journals is the contemplation of life's challenges, disappointments, and, most importantly, HOPE. Even in the darkest times, hope offers some comfort, purpose, and a willingness to see things differently.

In more recent times, journaling and diary writing has been associated with teenage girls, as depicted in glossy films and TV shows, but anyone who can write can use journaling to help set and meet goals, manage depression, or generally improve their quality of life. It is also being used in the treatment and recovery of post-traumatic stress disorder. [17]

There are lots of different ways to journal, and there are a huge number of resources online, but today's exercise is centered around positive journaling. Being able to remind yourself of positive or "hopeful" moments throughout the day can help reduce any lingering stress hormones from the day and help promote a good night's sleep.

Having a Positivity Journal doesn't mean you have to ignore negative moods and experiences. Instead, it enables you to see negative events as passing moments, in a similar way to noticing and letting go of thoughts while meditating, which then can be balanced in the present by recognizing positive experiences.

If the very thought of free writing terrifies you, you may wish to explore where this block has come from. Remember that writing down your thoughts is very different from writing something academic or coherent. Firstly, in most cases, you are the only one who will see it, and secondly, it only has to make sense to you. You don't need to be concerned with capitalization, punctuation, grammar, or spelling. Yippee! Just allow your thoughts to flow on the page without the need to follow any logic or rationality.

To help you get started, there is a useful acronym, WRITE, created by The Centre for Journal Therapy[18] which you might find useful if you feel you need more structure in your writing:

W - What do you feel like writing about?

R - Reflect on things that have happened from the point of how you feel.

I - Investigate what you are thinking and feeling. Are you feeling happy or tense?

T - Time yourself. Set a timer for five mins to start and build up to more in time.

E - Exit on purpose. Finish the process with a ritual, such as a mantra or breathing exercise.

Enjoy being creative with your thoughts, have fun with the progress, and just go with the flow.

TASK 7

For this activity, you will need a notebook/journal and a pen. This is best done first thing in the morning.

When you wake up, open your journal, and set a timer for 10 minutes. Repeat the word "HOPE" several times in your head and then free write in your journal any thoughts that arise. Just write. Don't worry about spelling or grammar, or whether what you are writing makes sense.

Aim to write about two to three pages on any thoughts that arise. Allow your mind to wander and go with the flow. When you find a natural pause or if you start to think logically about what to write, stop.

For an insightful read, check out: The Artist's Way: A Spiritual Path to Higher Creativity *by Julia Cameron* ☺

Journaling on Hope - Reflection

Take a moment to go over what you wrote in your journal. What did the word "hope" evoke in you? How did it feel at the time to write? Was it challenging, cathartic, frustrating, or soothing? Did you write a personal masterpiece, or did you just scrawl a mash of different thoughts and feelings on paper that had no chronological order or meaning?

There is no right or wrong way to journal, but if you struggled the first time, here are a few ideas that might help you get started or build momentum. First, identify why you are writing. Our exercise was centered around the word "hope", but you can use journaling to find answers, to de-clutter your mind, or simply to explore. If "blah, blah, blah" comes into your head, just write it down. There are no hard or fast rules!

You might find that your first attempt at writing feels like it doesn't make sense, and that's okay. There is a great benefit to be had from the repetitive nature of journaling, and sometimes it may take several attempts to understand what its purpose is for you. Each person's journey is unique.[19] Keep writing, and just try to let go without judgment and expectation.

Next steps

You have two options:

1. Schedule some time to write, either daily or a few times each week. If you wish, you can use a trigger word or ask yourself a question before you write and see if the answer flows to you. Work up to writing for 10-15 minutes for maximum benefit.

2. Write a few observational notes on what you discovered and move on to Day 8 with a new focus.

Whatever you decide, it is your journey towards building your self-awareness.

TAKE NOTE

WEEK ONE - REFLECTIONS

Use this section to recap on the past week

What resonated with you the most this week?

Which exercise did you find most challenging in week one and why?

How can you close the gap between where you are and where you want to be?

Further Reflections:

WEEK TWO – GETTING IN THE GROOVE

Congratulations on reaching week two of your 28 days of positivity. In the first week, each of the exercises centered around self-awareness. In this next week of positive activities, you will explore seven interventions that will help move your state from "meh" to "woohoo!"

This week is all about feeling good. Each of the lessons and activities is designed to enhance your state of wellbeing, increase your production of happy hormones, and make life worth living. Commit to the approach for each day, and feel free to extend the activity if you wish to. Remember, it is your journey towards feeling more positive, but take this opportunity to fully embrace and reflect on all the learnings these exercises have to offer and find what works for you.

Some interventions may resonate more than others, but as mentioned earlier, please try and persevere with any activity that you find yourself naturally repelling against, as you may just find the biggest growth here. Make a note of what is happening throughout, recording any highs and lows. Notice where your thoughts and feelings are throughout, and watch out for any internal dialogue that is attempting to give you a reality check by challenging your positivity.

Much of this week will focus on re-programming old negative thinking patterns and taking time to really appreciate who you are and where you are right now. At the beginning of the week, you will purposefully direct your thoughts towards a more positive outcome and feel what it is like to fully appreciate life and all the awesome things that surround you each and every day. Later in the week, you will have an opportunity to let your hair down (figuratively) and have a good hearty laugh, finding some freedom within to just be yourself in all your gorgeous goofiness.

Each of the interventions this week has been chosen to positively impact your mental health and wellbeing. Most can be slotted into your day pretty seamlessly, so if you feel the urge to continue with the exercise after the day is complete, it will easily fit alongside the other activities within the week.

If you feel in any way indulgent this week, embrace that feeling, capture it, and lean into it more. This week, be self-centered, feel indulgent, and embrace all of those things that make you go, "Oooh!"

DAY 8

Positive Affirmations

*"Cursing is an affirmation,
worrying is an affirmation,
and hatred is an affirmation...
You have the power to heal
your life… We always have the
power of our minds…Claim and
consciously use your power."*

– LOUISE HAY

Positive Affirmations

Are you a glass-half-full person? There have been lots of interesting research over the years that explores the effects of positive words and images. More recently, with the evolution of the field of neuroscience, it is now possible to see in real-time how the brain and body respond to certain suggestions and triggers.

The childhood phrase "sticks and stones may break my bones, but words can never hurt me" is a wonderful saying, but how true is it? Neuroscience shows that negative words can impact stress and anxiety-inducing hormones such as cortisol and adrenaline.[20] Not only that, but those negative words don't even have to be spoken or heard. Just thinking about negative words can cause you stress and, in some cases, can contribute to long-term anxiety and some illnesses. [21]

If you reflect back to day four, when you brought your focus to your internal dialogue, you will hopefully recognize the importance of being mindful of those beliefs which may be programmed or hard-wired in your brain. Today's exercise expands on this learning by identifying and intentionally reprogramming your brain to think differently.

Positive affirmations, also known as auto suggestions or positive mantras, are words or phrases that you can repetitively say to change your feelings or help influence a situation, unblocking limiting beliefs or negative habitual patterns. Words can have an even bigger impact when said with intent, so connecting with the feeling of each statement helps add extra potency to the words.

Thinking back to the phrase "words will never hurt me". This in itself could be recognized as a positive affirmation, but if you look at the composition of the phrase, two words pop out—"words" and "hurt". In its efforts to be an empowering statement, the brain may not comprehend it to be so. When compiling positive affirmations, it is important to look at the value of each word, so this could be rephrased as "words bring me strength and joy". Okay, you obviously have to use words that work for you, but hopefully, you get the point!

In 1999, Dr. Masaru Emoto published a number of works sharing his theory that water can be shaped by our thoughts, emotions and wider environment. During his studies, Emoto spoke to, wrote on, and played music to a variety of different water samples.[22] The vessels were then frozen and examined under a microscope. His results indicated that water holds memories just like a recorder, and as a result, each crystal changed its molecular structure depending on the message stated. For instance, the word "hate" made the crystals go murky and black in some cases.

The word "love" or "thank you" produced the finest, most beautiful crystalline structure.

Dr. Emoto's work is often replicated by amateur scientists using rice and water in jars which have been spoken to or written on, with lots of vlogs available to digest on YouTube and other social channels if you wish to explore more, or even give it a go yourself. The biggest takeaway from this is that, as humans are made up of an average of 60% water, we may need to pay a lot more attention to the words we think, say, and hear!

Today's technique therefore aims to raise your awareness and make a noticeable difference in how you process the information around you. Listen out for the noise that surrounds you that you are unaware of or listening to. Do you regularly listen to or read bad news online on the TV or radio? Are there people around you who are constantly negative? What can you do to minimize the impact of external negative influences?

On day eight, start with you and remember that repetition and intent are key. For instance, if you are running late, stating the words "I have all the time I need" repetitively may make the difference between you arriving late in a panic or walking in on time, calm and confident. Try it and see.

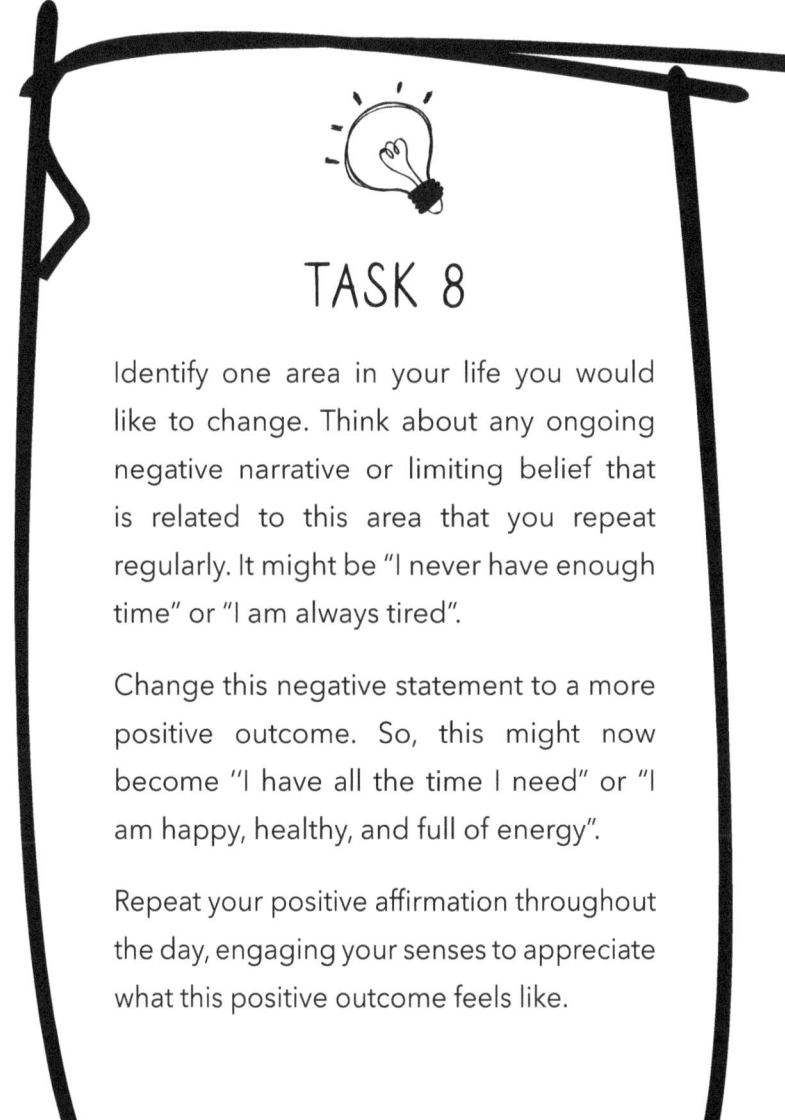

TASK 8

Identify one area in your life you would like to change. Think about any ongoing negative narrative or limiting belief that is related to this area that you repeat regularly. It might be "I never have enough time" or "I am always tired".

Change this negative statement to a more positive outcome. So, this might now become "I have all the time I need" or "I am happy, healthy, and full of energy".

Repeat your positive affirmation throughout the day, engaging your senses to appreciate what this positive outcome feels like.

For an encouraging read, check out: The Power of Your Subconscious Mind *by Joseph Murphy* 😊

Reframing Negativity - Reflection

What did you discover when you changed your limiting belief to something more positive? What thoughts were going on in your head at the time? Did any negative or rational thoughts creep in? It is quite common to initially experience negative dialogue in response to positive affirmations. Your mind may go into rational talk trying to convince you that this is not real. If this happens, thank and congratulate yourself for your inner protection mechanism, and continue on with your affirmations.

Positive affirmations or positive inner dialogue are integral to behavioral change and may be essential to your ongoing wellbeing.[23] Throughout week one, you will have built awareness of your thoughts, feelings, and behaviors, and now it is your chance to start reprogramming what you want to think, feel, and experience. When you engaged your senses alongside doing the affirmation, how did that feel? While this exercise works best when you use it repetitively over several weeks, it is also possible that you noticed an instant response following your first application of this concept. Make sure you take notes and make every effort to fit this practice in whenever you can, and see if anything changes for you over time.

Next steps

You have two options:

1. For an extra boost, write your affirmations on post-it notes around your house or work environment and repeat them regularly with intent each time you see them for the remaining days in this book.

2. Write a few observational notes on what you discovered and move on to Day 9 with a new focus.

Whatever you decide, it is your journey this week towards feeling good.

TAKE NOTE

DAY 9

Gratitude

"Gratitude is one of the strongest and most transformative states of being. It shifts your perspective from lack to abundance and allows you to focus on the good in your life, which in turn pulls more goodness into your reality."

– JEN SINCERO

Gratitude

How grateful are you? If you explore the science of gratitude, you may discover that it is pretty hard to define. To some, it is perceived as a behavior, a feeling, or an emotion, while others define it as a trait or a virtue. You might see it as something that was drummed into you as a child when you were constantly being told to say "Thank you" or appreciate what was around you (although you will appreciate the value of that very soon!).

Gratitude means different things to different people. It has been coined in research as the "social glue" that connects society.[24] It is often personified, even in the instances where we offer gratitude for the weather or "fate's hand". Even non-religious people have been heard to say, "Thank God!"

Studies on gratitude over the last few decades have demonstrated that being thankful is more than just good manners, a warm feeling, or positive thinking. In positive psychology it has been demonstrated through many studies that being thankful not only makes you a lot happier but can also reduce stress and burnout, make you more resilient, and improve cardiovascular health.[25]

The extraordinary thing about gratitude is that, when fully embraced, it can stop anxiety, fear, or worry in its tracks. That's right, the brain cannot actually respond to gratitude and anxiety at the same time, due to both reactions stemming from the same neurotransmitters in the brain. These neurotransmitters are responsible for sending out important chemical messages to the body. By intentionally focusing on all that is good around you, through gratitude, you are weakening any potential habits of naturally reacting to all the bad stuff that is around you. Be patient as you develop your skills of looking for the good, and know that you are not ignoring your potentially dire situation, but rather you are choosing to see things differently.

Spending some time to observe how much time you give to gratitude over the course of a day is a great starting point. Think of how it feels when someone out of the blue thanks you for something that you really didn't expect to be thanked for. How does it feel? What emotions does it bring up for you? Monitor if you accept the appreciation, or do you deflect it? Many people fall into the habit of deflecting the gift of gratitude by replying with "Ah, it was nothing", "no problem", "not a biggy", etc. If this is something you do, attempt to catch yourself next time and change your response to fully accepting and savoring the appreciation. It will be a different experience.

Gratitude and appreciation can be expressed in a number of different ways. A simple activity such as saying "Thank you" as you acknowledge when someone has done something for you is really good to start off with, but making a more conscious effort to be grateful during the day can make a huge difference to your mood and life outcomes.

Martin Seligman, who is also known as the Father of Positive Psychology and an expert in happiness, has carried out a number of research projects on the benefits of gratitude.[26] One of his studies looked at writing down three things (people, places, or things) that you are grateful for and then recalling why you are grateful for these things, noting this down in detail.

With this in mind try and embody the experience of gratitude today in this next exercise and appreciate every moment as you write and reflect. This gratitude exercise can be used as an extension of the journal work you did on day seven. In fact, you can use your journal to document your three things each day. When you practice gratitude with awareness, you may notice that you start to find more and more things to be grateful for. Try it out and see where it leads you!

TASK 9

You will need a notepad or your journal for this exercise.

Before going to bed at night, recall and write down three things you are grateful for that happened that day. Now, reflect on why you are grateful for these things and write your thoughts down.

Finally, take some time to embrace the happiest or most gratifying parts of the day. Bask in these things you feel most grateful for, in your mind, by visualizing yourself enjoying them. Have a wonderful sleep!

For a gratifying read, check out: The Gratitude Diaries: How a Year Looking on the Bright Side Can Transform Your Life *by Janice Kaplan* ☺

Embracing Gratitude - Reflection

How did it feel to take time to appreciate and savor three things that you are truly grateful for at the end of the evening? Perhaps this is an exercise you have done before, and you are a naturally appreciative person, but maybe you have realized that you rarely take the time to feel grateful for and appreciate those little and big things around you.

If you find it challenging to find things you feel grateful for, that's okay. Rather than waiting until the evening, it may be quite beneficial to look out for things to be grateful for throughout the day, such as the sun shining on your face, your first coffee in the morning, or a stranger smiling at you. Observing yourself and your response to experiencing gratitude is also an interesting aspect of this exercise.

For some people, negative bias can blind them to the amazing things surrounding them. If this is you, try and replace any negativity with something that you can appreciate. This is a particularly good exercise for improving relationships that might be challenging. Always look for the good, no matter how hidden it may appear.

Next steps

You have two options:

1. You may extend this exercise by adding it to your daily wellbeing routine and reflecting on things you are most grateful for in different categories, such as: I am so happy and grateful for these things: in my work, in my family, in the world, etc.

2. Write a few observational notes on what you discovered and move on to Day 10 with a new focus.

Whatever you decide, it is your journey this week towards feeling good.

TAKE NOTE

DAY 10

Savoring

"Learn to enjoy every minute of your life. Be happy now. Don't wait for something outside of yourself to make you happy in the future. Think how really precious is the time you have to spend, whether it's at work or with your family. Every minute should be enjoyed and savored."

– EARL NIGHTINGALE

Savoring

How aware are you when you eat your food? Have you ever snatched a bite to eat during lunch "on the go" or while you are working at your computer? Maybe you eat on the move while rushing out in the morning or find yourself exhausted in the evening and eat while watching TV or a good movie. You might have even occasionally asked yourself, "Did I eat that?" as you were so focused on something else, you were oblivious to the half packet of biscuits you just devoured! Everyone has a very individual approach to food. You might find food comforting or use it to connect with family and/or friends. A common trait, though, in modern society is that people rarely pause before eating or take a moment to fully appreciate the value of the food they consume. As a result, your relationship with food may become tainted, and at worst, it can make you overweight or even very ill.

You may be familiar with the term "savoring" when it comes to food, and the focus today will be just that: adopting the process of savoring everything you eat. As you can fit this easily into your daily routine, this may be the perfect activity to continue your exploration of building awareness within, giving you the opportunity to uncover any judgment or emotional connection you may be projecting onto your food. Savoring enables you to bring your full awareness to an object, place, experience, person, or food, so you can fully appreciate and enjoy everything there is about it. Known as an "active behavior", savoring - and following on from last week's theme: awareness - is an important part of that cog.

The food you put into your body is integral to your health and wellbeing. It can make the difference between feeling energetic and sluggish. Then there is the weight factor that excessive food can influence. With savoring, you can start to increase awareness of what you are eating and become more conscious of your choice of food and drink. Essentially, savoring helps you slow down. It allows you to enjoy everything you consume and begin to feel good about what you are putting in your body, which ultimately benefits your physical and mental wellbeing.[27]

When you feel that the food you are consuming is going to be good for you, your brain will carry this information to the rest of your body to help reaffirm its benefits. We often spend so much time eating the wrong foods and reprimanding ourselves before, during, or after we eat. Have you ever said to yourself, "I really shouldn't eat this", or "I know this is really bad for me", or "I really shouldn't have eaten that"? In this exercise, you will start to approach your food more mindfully and savor everything you eat today, both the healthy and the potentially less healthy stuff. What you might find is that you start to opt for the more nutritious foods.

You may also wish to add some positive statements along with the process, using your knowledge from day eight, such as "This is delicious', or 'This food is nourishing and great for my health". You might additionally express gratitude for your food, thanking it and appreciating how it makes you feel. Think back to Dr. Emoto's water experiment and consider how much water is contained in the foods you eat. If you do decide to eat something that you feel might not be overly beneficial for your health, such as that large slice of chocolate cake, then try changing the narrative - enjoy every mouthful and appreciate how it makes you feel. Avoid any guilt afterwards by affirming to yourself. "This cake is greatly beneficial for my emotional health and is nourishing for me." You may not believe this if you do it too often, but on occasion and in balance, there is still a great benefit. Enjoy!

TASK 10

When eating today, first engage all your senses before you take a bite. Check out the texture and color–perhaps it is glistening. Smell your food. What aroma does it have? Put it in your mouth and notice what it feels like before you bite into it. When in your mouth, slowly chew, identifying each of the flavors that you can taste. Enjoy the process and slowly chew around 30 times before you swallow.

What do you feel about this food? Do you have any emotional connection to it? What is your inner voice saying? If your narrative is negative, try and consider some positive things to say about your food.

For a scrumptious read, check out: Savor: Mindful Eating, Mindful Life *by Thich Nhat Hanh and Lilian Cheung* ☺

Savoring Your Food - Reflection

How many times in one day did you remember to apply the savoring exercise when eating food? If you managed to do it at least once, was the experience any different from how you normally eat? If so, what specifically was different? Did you feel any emotional connection to your food? Did you notice any thoughts present at the time?

A number of biological things happen to you as you savor your food. When you remain present when eating (that is, you spend time noticing and enjoying each bite of food you are consuming), you will digest better, feel fuller quicker and potentially aid in weight loss.[28]

It is quite common for people to rush or consume food without fully noticing or appreciating why they are eating the food in the first place. Spending just 10 minutes fully focused when eating can make a huge difference to your mental and physical health. So, before you eat, pause, observe, and then enjoy!

Next steps

You have two options:

1. Make a conscious effort to pause before you
    eat over this coming week. Continue to monitor
    those thoughts and feelings that arise before,
    during, and after you eat. You may also start to
    look for other things to savor, such as time with
    loved ones, positive memories, a compliment
    you received, etc.

2. Write a few observational notes on what you
    discovered and move on to Day 11 with a new
    focus.

Whatever you decide, it is your journey this week
towards feeling good.

TAKE NOTE

DAY II

Behind the Mirror

"If you're searching for that one person who will change your life... take a look in the mirror."

– UNKNOWN

Behind the Mirror

Who is the person staring back at you from behind your mirror? What do they say to you when you pause to reflect on what you see? Are they always complimentary, or do they barrage you with comments that suggest you don't look quite right, you are flawed, too fat, too skinny, or simply not good enough? If your closest friend was behind this reflective glass and said to you any of these things that you catch yourself saying, would you accept it? If not, then why would you put up with it yourself?

There is a multitude of studies and research centered around the benefits of mirror play on young children's development.[29] Mirrors can help develop self-awareness, emotional security, and self-regulation. If you are a parent or have watched a baby playing, you may have experienced the delight of a young face when they see their reflection in the mirror or something shiny. There is no judgment, no criticism, and no disgust. The experience is one of awe, delight, and fascination.

From six months, babies start to interact with the face behind a mirror by smiling, babbling, or touching the glass. By 16 months, babies can start to recognize their reflection, and they may begin to imitate and react visibly to what they see. They will start to play with sounds, facial expressions, and body movements and may even kiss themselves as a gesture of acceptance.

All the way through infancy and childhood, children continue their relationship with mirrors, regularly checking in with themselves when they are looking for reassurance or self-acceptance. By the time they become teenagers, and their cell phone cameras become a valuable portable addition to the mirror, something shifts. Self-acceptance and reassurance may now be challenged by self-criticism and negative talk. Depending on a person's home and peer environment, this can come a lot sooner. By the time a child reaches young adulthood, the mirror (or camera) can become a way to abuse, to highlight all the imperfections and flaws; to program unkind messages and taunts, often unconsciously, that we would simply not accept from anybody else.

In today's exercise, you are encouraged to stand in front of the mirror and spend some time just looking at yourself while listening to the inner dialogue that comes back. Is your self-talk complimentary and encouraging? Or are you making any unnecessary judgments about yourself? Maybe nothing is coming back to you, as it is simply not what you have ever considered.

This simple activity today can be used daily or whenever you see a mirror. Perhaps when brushing your teeth or if you are applying make-up, shaving, or drying your hair. Or more purposefully, every time you wash your hands.

As you will have learned in day eight's activity, neuroscience has shown that regularly repeating positive statements can literally change the structure of the brain and reprogram a person's perception of themselves. So, ask yourself, do you love and accept all parts of yourself when you look in the mirror? Do you look at yourself with the same eyes as you did when you were a toddler, in awe, delight, and fascination? If not, why not? What has shifted for you over the years? Are you holding on to something from the past that is blocking you for remembering and seeing the real you? Try exploring some mirror play, resisting any urge to judge yourself along the way, and see what happens ;-)

TASK II

In a comfortable, relaxed space, take some time to look at yourself in a mirror. Spend five minutes just exploring yourself without judgment.

Now, with a gentle smile on your face, say to yourself, "I love you, and I accept you." If you discover that your inner critic is being very vocal, stick with it and keep repeating the phrase.

If you feel this is challenging or you feel uncomfortable, consider changing the phrase to "I am willing to love and accept you".

Be open with yourself and take as long as you need to really see yourself without any filters.

For a reflective read, check out: Mirror Work: 21 Days to Heal Your Life *by Louise Hay* ☺

Mirror Exercise - Reflection

When a person is faced with their face staring back through a mirror, it can go a couple of ways. So, ask yourself how this exercise went. Did you have a "meh" moment, or catch an occasion where you thought, "Yeah, I look great", or perhaps you started a spiral of criticism, be it a misplaced freckle, a crooked feature, or a furrowed line?

What was the inner dialogue that was going on for you? Did this dialogue change when you announced to yourself, 'I love you'? How did this feel? Have you ever told yourself this before? What was your response to this self-declaration?

Did you feel nothing? Were you confused at the point of the exercise? Or did you feel uncomfortable? If you experienced any of these reactions, try and do the exercise again. Using positive affirmations in front of the mirror can add to the potency of the words you use. Aim to sit with any discomfort you experience and enjoy learning to love yourself inside and out.

Next steps

You have two options:

1. To increase the impact of this exercise, use any mirror time as an opportunity to stop, look, and appreciate what you see. Make a point of pausing before and after washing your hands, brushing your teeth, or combing your hair. You could also write positive statements to yourself in the mirror to serve as a reminder throughout your day.

2. Write a few observational notes on what you discovered and move on to Day 12 with a new focus.

Whatever you decide, it is your journey this week towards feeling good.

TAKE NOTE

DAY 12

Laughter

"The human race has one really effective weapon, and that is laughter."

– MARK TWAIN

Laughter Yoga

What's so funny? You have probably heard the saying "laughter is the best medicine", but where did it come from, and what does it mean? This reference to laughter dates back to the 1300s when a professor of surgery found that laughter was an effective way to induce pain-free sleep following an operation.[30] He discovered that 10 minutes of laughter allowed patients to get two hours of pain-free sleep. Since then, laughter has been used as a method to improve wellbeing, reduce burnout, and stop anxiety in its tracks. As a natural pain suppressor, it is also pretty effective during labor and childbirth.

Laughter releases happy hormones such as oxytocin, dopamine, endorphins, and serotonin, in addition to reducing stress hormones such as cortisol and adrenalin. Studies have shown that laughing for up to 15 minutes a day can help break negative thinking patterns, improving depression, insomnia, and high blood pressure.[31] But how can we tap into this free and amazing tool? Simple things like enjoying comedy on TV, listening to a funny podcast, or watching animal videos on YouTube might help, but you could also try out laughter therapy or laughter yoga.

Laughter yoga was first introduced by Dr. Madan Kataria in 1995 with just five people and a lot of jokes.

When the jokes ran out, Dr. Katarina explored the effect of tricking the body with intentional laughter, which started to produce the same effects as spontaneous laughter. The results were a huge success, and laughter yoga was born, combining laughter exercises, breathing techniques, stretching, and lots of playfulness. In just 30 years, the concept has grown exponentially, with over 10,000 clubs now worldwide. [32]

An important thing to recognize is that the mind and body can't always tell the difference between fake laughter and a real one. Therefore, if you purposefully create a cycle of laughter, the benefits could be the same as having a good giggle while watching a movie. You still release those lovely hormones, and you still get the benefits. In fact, the University of Michigan calculated that just 20 seconds of hearty laughter could be as good for the lungs as a short workout.[33] It also rapidly reduces stress and anxiety and boosts your immune system.

In today's exercise, you will explore a couple of laughter placements. You may already recognize the difference between a 'chuckle', or slightly suppressed laugh and a hearty "belly" laugh, but can you identify any patterns in your laughing behavior? If you watch a young baby giggle, you may notice that their whole body gets involved. There is a wonderful statistic that states young children laugh around 400 times per day, and yet adults only manage to have a chuckle a pitiful 15 times per day.[34]

Can you remember the last time you had a good laugh? Think about the people around you, including those who live with you or whom you interact with on a daily basis. How often do they laugh? What makes them laugh? What do you notice when they laugh? Does their laughing have an effect on you? What happens to your body when you laugh? How does this change, depending on the intensity of the laughter?

There are some wonderful resources online to show you how to maximize the effectiveness of your laughter, but the exercise today will offer a small introduction to laughter placement. Do it with a friend, embrace that belly laugh, be loud and be playful. Enjoy this exercise and spread the joy. It can be very contagious!!!

TASK 12

Stand up with your feet hip-width apart. Place your hand on your throat, take a deep breath into your diaphragm as we explored on day two, and as you exhale, make the sound "He, He, He".

Now place your hand on your chest or your heart area. Again, take a deep breath and make the sound "Ha, Ha, Ha", while breathing out.

For the final stage, place your hand on your tummy and make the sound "Ho, Ho, Ho", using your full breath on the sound. Repeat the exercise for a full 10 minutes. Observe what thoughts and feelings arise.

For a hilarious read, check out: Laughter Yoga: Daily Laughter Practices for Health and Happiness *by Dr Madan Kataria* ☺

Laughter Yoga - Reflection

The big question following this exercise is, did it make you laugh? For some people, the simple act of placing the sounds where you often feel laughter is enough to set them off in a fit of giggles. If this didn't happen to you, don't worry, as you can practice it at any time and (almost) any place. Just "fake it until you make it" and have fun with it!

Connecting with others to do the exercise alongside you may help uncover something hilarious lurking within you. You could also look at some funny videos of animals or of babies laughing to inspire you to crack up and let out a hearty roar.

If you are a little out of practice with laughing, make it your mission for the rest of the week to find the humor in everyday things, and before long, you will be clocking up your 400 laughs each day in no time. Keep laughing!

Next steps

You have two options:

1. Repeat this exercise daily if it works for you and try and get friends or family involved. Join your local Laughter Club in person or online. It's free or of very low cost, and you'll be guaranteed to have a good laugh at least once or twice a month!

2. Write a few observational notes on what you discovered and move on to Day 13 with a new focus.

Whatever you decide, it is your journey this week towards feeling good.

TAKE NOTE

DAY 13

Your Song

"Sometimes music is the only medicine the heart and soul need."

– UNKNOWN

Your Song

Do you "own" your own song? This is possibly the simplest activity in this book and one that you may already do. If you listen to music often, what kind of music evokes the biggest emotional response in you? Is it happy or sad music you most enjoy listening to? Is it the lyrics or the melody that most resonates?

If you recall back to day eight again and Dr. Emoto's study on water (where the spoken and written word influences the frozen molecular structure of water), well, you may not be surprised that so does music. Music such as John Lennon's Imagine or Beethoven's Pastoral produced beautiful crystalline structures, whereas heavy metal created a fragmented, distorted mass. Just like Bridget in the opening scene of "Bridget Jones's Diary", when she feels doomed to ever find love and personifies Celine Dion's song "All by Myself" to feed her loneliness, we, as humans, love to embrace music to reflect or change our emotions, feelings, and mood, both in sadness and in joy.

Sad music, however, is not all that bad. Both sad and happy music have been shown to release the neurotransmitters and happy hormones, dopamine, and serotonin, which are responsible for pleasure and regulation.[35] Listening to sad music may increase your capacity to ruminate on your problems or to search for solutions, so while it can enable you to mentally heal and recover, it can also keep you stuck.

Scientific research has demonstrated the extraordinary power of music on the body and mind, with evidence to show that some music can lower blood pressure, decrease your heart rate, boost the immune system, build self-esteem, and reduce anxiety. Music therapy is a growing field that is now being used medically, including in the physical and cognitive recovery of stroke patients; enabling Alzheimer's patients to communicate better with loved ones, and in some surgeries to minimize pain and to induce quicker recovery.[36,37]

With the development of neuroscience, scientists are able to see the effects of music and sound frequency in real time through brain imaging. The frequency of the sound can also have a positive impact on your brain health, influencing how your brain waves behave. When you listen to calm, slow, relaxing music, it can move you from the "beta state", which is known as the "awake" or "active brain state", to the "alpha state", which relaxes your focus, reduces stress, and evokes positive thinking. The alpha state can also be recognized as the moment between being awake or asleep and moving through these stages of brain state are usually involuntary.

Binaural beats have been used for some time to help influence and move through these brain waves more intentionally. First discovered around the mid 1800s by Heinrich Wilheim Dome, it wasn't until 1973 that these beats were commercialized and used as a mainstream intervention within music tracks with these beats hidden within. The most common music with a binaural beat is that which is used for meditation. This type of music aims to purposefully move a person from beta to alpha and eventually theta, promoting deep relaxation and REM sleep. Alpha and theta brain states can be an optimum time for reprogramming your brain through positive affirmations or auto-suggestion. Guided meditation tracks regularly use music alongside positive affirmations to guide you through these positive restorative brain states to induce favorable outcomes.

Whether you use music to relax or energize you, the most exciting part in all of this is that just imagining music playing in your head can induce similar restorative brain activity. Today's activity, however, does not aim to put you into a slumber or pensive state but rather to induce a feeling of positivity, connection, and intense joy. As this is your journey, feel free to have a play and see what works best for you!

TASK 13

Find a happy, positive song that you absolutely love and play it at a volume slightly louder than normal but still safe for your ears. You can also play this song with headphones.

Standing up, "own" this song as if it was created just for you. Sing it (if it has lyrics), hum it, move, sway, jump, or throw yourself (safely) around the room.

Feel this music embody every part of your being. When it finishes, sit down with your eyes closed, and feel the energy and power within you.

Smile and go along with your day.

For a soulful read, check out: This Is Your Brain on Music: Understanding a Human Obsession *by Daniel Levitin* ☺

Owning Your Song - Reflection

It is no surprise that music can influence your cognitive cycle of thinking, feeling, and behaving, but did you notice this cycle while you were engaging with your song? When you sat down and closed your eyes at the end of the song, what could you feel happening in your body? Did you feel tired, elated, or tingly?

What was your face saying? If someone came into the room and saw you following the end of this exercise, how might they have perceived you? Were there any images present in your head, either before, during, or after the song? If so, did these in any way influence the way you felt or behaved?

Now the big question is: Was one song enough? Did the exercise make you want more, or were you happy just with this single interaction? Try to recall all of the feelings and emotions that surfaced during and after the exercise. Did it make you think differently? What did you do after the exercise? How long did the feeling last?

Next steps

You have two options:

1. Set aside some time each morning to set up your day positively and choose three powerfully positive tracks to dance to, sing to, and embody, ending with a quiet moment of gratitude for the feeling they bring.

2. Write a few observational notes on what you discovered and move on to Day 14 with a new focus.

Whatever you decide, it is your journey this week towards feeling good.

TAKE NOTE

DAY 14

Walking in Nature

"Look deep into nature, and then you will understand everything better."

– ALBERT EINSTEIN

Walking in Nature

When was the last time you took a walk in nature? It is no great surprise that nature and natural elements are your body's greatest healer. When people are ill, a common response might be to suggest that they "get some fresh air", or "get out in the open". Fresh air is not just what it is about, though; the very connection of spending time in or near nature can improve mental, physical, and spiritual wellbeing. Walking in nature is an activity that attracts a great deal of research, notably showing that being outdoors can reduce stress by lowering cortisol (the "fight or flight" hormone), diminishing depressive symptoms, and increasing motivation.[38]

How you behave and what you do outside can also have an impact on your mental health. If you go for a walk outside and don't necessarily feel any better about it, ask yourself if you are truly present when you are out. Whether you are walking for fitness, going for a stroll, hiking, or walking the dog, look out for any habits that might be occurring as you are walking. Where do you direct your attention: out to the vast open space, focusing on the detail of every living thing, or do you look at your feet? What is your body doing: are you breathing in deeply, springing with every step, or are you hunched over, dodging both foliage and flies with every breeze?

What is your relationship with nature? Do you have any barriers which might be blocking you from experiencing nature's full delights? While today's exercise involves taking a walk in nature, you can experience the benefits of nature without walking. Engaging your senses as you smell some flowers, watch an army of ants collecting food, listen to the bird song, taste some wild blackberries, or feel the softness of the grass beneath your bare feet.

You don't always have to "be at one" with open green space. Perhaps you are a little fearful of being on your own in more secluded natural spaces. If this sounds like you, can you pinpoint where this fear is coming from? If you could do just one thing to make yourself feel better in nature, what would it be?

If greenery isn't your thing, consider taking yourself to the seaside, where statistically, people who live there experience 22% fewer mental health issues.[39] If you fancy a swim in the sea on your visit, you can expect to experience a super endorphin dose to melt all your troubles away and enjoy a detoxifying treatment of potassium, magnesium, calcium, and iodine, akin to an expensive spa treatment. But, simply walking in the sand barefoot will still work wonders. As you listen to the sound of the waves coming in and away from the shore, breathe in the enriched oxygen sea air deep into your lungs, and discover wonderful treasures poking up from the sand and hidden between the rocks.

The outdoors is generally a perfect place to start interacting socially if it has been a while since you met up with friends. Even with strangers, nature can act as a wonderful conversation point! If you feel you need support with this exercise, ask a friend or family member to do this activity with you. What might it feel like to engage with nature while you have company? How would your relationship with both people and nature change? Walking mindfully outside, taking in the sights, sounds, and smells in any nature-rich environment will boost your energy levels, lift your mood, and enhance your awareness. Breathing slowly as you walk and widening your focus can both help enhance your experience.

TASK 14

Today, take a walk out in nature. Be prepared to give nature your time, and don't rush.

Instead of walking with a fixed focus or looking around, just widen your view without focusing on anything in particular— as if you were looking through the wide-angle, panoramic lens of a camera. Just take it all in as if you were looking at a beautiful landscape picture.

Feel how different it is to walk, fully taking in the full experience of your surroundings and immersing yourself in the wondrous awe of nature.

For a wondrous read, check out: The Wild Remedy: How Nature Mends Us - A Diary *by Emma Mitchell* 🙂

Taking a Walk in Nature - Reflection

On day 14, you were encouraged to take a walk in nature and try and re-frame your perspective. What did you discover? Were you able to keep your focus wide, or were you drawn to individual aspects of your walk? When you started to walk, where did you look? Ahead? Around? At your feet?

Did you have the urge to do anything else on your walk, such as look at your phone or listen to music? If so, was this out of habit, through a moment of discomfort, or both? Be mindful of when you have the compulsion to do something which takes your full focus away from the task at hand. Even something as benign as listening to music could be your body's way of signaling you to return to your "comfort zone".

Did you notice any inner dialogue going on during your walk, or were you able to fully immerse yourself in the experience? Did you gain any further insights that you feel are valuable to include in your journal? Next time you take a walk, observe closely what happens.

Next steps

You have two options:

1. Go one step further and enjoy forest bathing (known as Shinrin-yoku in Japan), engaging all your senses (sight, sound, smell, taste, and touch) while walking slowly through a forest for two hours, or take a foraging course for a fully immersive experience!

2. Write a few observational notes on what you discovered and move on to Day 15 with a new focus.

Whatever you decide, it is your journey this week towards feeling good.

TAKE NOTE

WEEK TWO - REFLECTIONS

Use this section to recap on the past week.

What resonated with you the most this week?

Which exercise did you find most challenging in week two and why?

How can you close the gap between where you are and where you want to be?

Further Reflections:

WEEK THREE -
YOUR POWER OF INFLUENCE

Y ou may have heard the saying, "You can't change other people", but what if you could change how people see you? It can take just one-tenth of a second for someone to form an opinion about you, even before you meet. Unfortunately, what we are thinking and feeling at the time of meeting someone can have a real impact on how we are perceived by the other individual. For example, if you are feeling insecure, confident, happy, or worried, this might be picked up by the other person in your facial expressions, your body language, and even your voice.

Week three considers those areas of influence you have on others through intentional behaviors. Building from those foundations you learned in weeks one and two, you will become increasingly aware of how you present yourself to others so you can start to shape how others perceive you. This can be as effective in social settings as it is in work settings.

To help you understand a bit better what might be happening from another's perspective, consider how you perceive others when you meet them for the first time, or perhaps you can reflect on interacting with someone who challenges you in some way. This week, monitor what judgments you formulate when you meet different categories of people, such as friends, colleagues, strangers, or those who share different values or virtues, etc. What criteria do you use to form your opinion?

In week three, you will explore some techniques that encourage you to listen and speak more impactfully. You will consider the lens through which you are noticing others, and you will practice kindness and compassion with those around you. Take lots of mental and physical notes this week, closely observing any changes in the way some people start to behave around you.

This week is all about connecting with yourself and others, exploring and observing as you go. If you don't normally have many interactions with others, make it your purpose to go out more this week, where you can meet other individuals and try out the activities with colleagues, strangers, friends, or with family. People need to be connected, and this innate need for social connectedness has been long linked to better health, wellbeing, and emotional regulation.

Humans are social creatures that draw energy from each other, but are you an energy booster or an energy vampire? Throughout this week, you will have the opportunity to recognize the impact you can have on others and explore ways to positively influence those you know and love, along with those you are not overly fond of, and also complete strangers. Have fun with the exercises and take lots of notes!

DAY 15

Vocal Connection

"The sweetest music is not in the oratorio, but in the human voice when it speaks from its instant life tones of tenderness, truth, or courage."

– RALPH WALDO EMERSON

Vocal Connection

What does your voice say about you? In 2017, a study by Yale discovered that the human race is heavily influenced by the sound of someone's voice, even much more than sight.[40] This serves as a great reminder, highlighting how the quality of a person's voice can shape how another person might feel. In the same way that a calm voice might soothe you or someone's raised voice makes you feel stressed, the quality and tone of the voice are essential indicators as to what is happening beneath.

First impressions are also important. It can take less than a second for us to judge whether someone is trustworthy after meeting them or even without seeing them![41] This type of judgment may aim to protect you and keep you safe, but it can prove incredibly unhelpful if your judgments are driving your emotions. Consider the outcomes of being driven by strong emotions when attending an interview, standing up to deliver a speech, or trying to calm a child having a tantrum! Today, your exploration of voice is not just about discovering how you influence others, as we will be placing equal emphasis on how the quality of your voice may be impacting how you feel.

Every time you speak, an intention will lurk behind the words, often driven by an emotional response.

As covered earlier in the book, for every thought that you think or word that you say, you will have a corresponding feeling or emotion. This may be a conscious or subconscious process. Remember also that for every feeling or emotion that you experience, you will have a corresponding behavior, and this is what influences others and can impact how you feel. Thus, the cycle continues. For instance, if someone asks you to do something you don't want to do, you may think, "I don't want to do this." The feelings might be conflict and discomfort. However, you might choose to say, "Sure, no problem," because you don't wish to upset someone. What do you think the corresponding behavior might be? What does your body language say? What is your face saying that your words are not? What has happened to your tone and quality of voice?

This type of conflict can happen in a variety of scenarios. It is quite common for a person to try and hide their honesty and feelings of discomfort, insecurity, and fear. However, all this has an influence on your vocal quality, and, in some cases, if you have suppressed your real feelings for a long period of time, it can start to develop into a limiting personality trait. Monitoring your patterns of vocal behavior can be the first step towards change. Awareness of the space you are speaking into, and breathing is key to enabling the voice to share its full resonance.

Before we get into today's exercise, hold your hand up close to your face, about three to five inches away, as if you were closely reading a menu. Now, just focus on that hand. You may notice that your breathing has gone much shallower, or you might even notice that you're holding your breath because the space is so small. This is a great exercise to illustrate how people can restrict their breath and their voice, often subconsciously, to fit the space they are in. So, if you are feeling confined, either physically in a small space or emotionally feeling trapped or conflicted, your voice may correspond accordingly.

Today's exercise introduces you to a technique to release the voice and to use the physical space you are in, allowing you to focus on the external space rather than the internal space, getting you out of your head and into the present moment. Like with everything in this book, practice and repetition are key. Watch the impact on the quality of the voice as you practice, and particularly note how it makes you feel. You may also wish to audio record this activity and see if anything changes with your voice over time.

TASK 15

Start this activity by standing up in a small space. Say aloud, "I hold great power in my voice." Notice what this sounds like and where your voice is coming from.

Now, place your hand on your abdomen, just above your belly button. Focus far out into a large space. If you are not in a large space, just imagine being able to see through the wall and way out into the distance.

Sense the space all around you as you breathe in deeply into your abdomen. As you exhale, say, "I hold great power in my voice," this time sending the sound out into the expanded space. How did the sound differ?

For a resonant read, check out: The Power of Voice: A Guide to Making Yourself Heard *by Denise Woods* ☺

Finding Your Voice - Reflection

When you completed the vocal exercise, and sent your sound far beyond the space, what happened to your voice? Hopefully, you have begun to understand how your voice is affected by the space you are in. If you recorded the exercise, you might have noticed a difference in the quality of your voice, and not just with the sound and volume. What changed when you connected with your breath and re-adjusted your focus on the space? What were your biggest take-aways from this simple exercise?

Continue to notice when and if your voice changes during specific circumstances, situations, or with people, that challenge you. Reflect on what happened and what was said. What were you thinking? What were your emotions and feelings at the time? Was there anything you might have done differently? Is there anything you can learn from this? Could you approach this type of circumstance, situation, or person with a new lens next time? When you get the opportunity, practice this new intentional voice on others and notice if there is any change in how they respond to you.

Next steps

You have two options:

1. Soon after you wake up each morning, spend some time using the breathing space exercise to warm up your voice. If you record this activity every day, you can monitor any improvements in your vocal quality as you move through the weeks.

2. Write a few observational notes on what you discovered and move on to Day 16 with a new focus.

Whatever you decide, it is your journey towards extending your power of influence.

TAKE NOTE

DAY 16

Active Listening

"Listening doesn't always equate to hearing. Hearing doesn't always lead to understanding, but active listening helps each person truly 'see' the other."

– SANJO JENDAYI

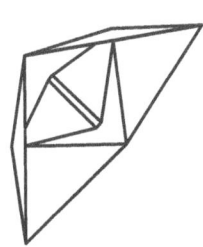

Active Listening

Are you a good listener? You may by now have started to recognize a bit of a theme in that most exercises in this book encourage you to take more notice of the automated things you do each and every day. You might wonder why this is necessary. Well, some neuroscientists suggest that the average human can spend 95% of their waking day in the process of automation.[42] While breathing is something you may be pretty happy to be automated, listening might be a task that you would benefit from having a little more control over.

With the increase in technology use and disruptions to socialization due to the pandemic, might you have lost the art of communicating actively and empathetically? To gauge the degree of this, reflect on whether, in conversation with another person, you are truly engaged with what they are saying or if your thoughts are elsewhere.

Today's activity looks (or sounds) like active listening. Lack of listening is one of the biggest reasons for the breakdown of relationships. If you ever find yourself struggling to keep quiet while your partner, family member, or child is talking, as you are keen to "help", put your point across, or "hurry up" the conversation, then this exercise might really benefit you. It is also hugely beneficial in the work environment.

Regardless of your intent behind your "active talking" in conversations, taking the time to truly listen to another person shows them that you acknowledge their opinion and appreciate their thoughts and feelings. By validating the other person's emotions instead of offering advice, you demonstrate empathy while also helping them feel valued.

In a work context, if you have the habit of talking and leading conversations, be aware of the ways in which you may be influencing others. Do others engage actively in the conversation? Are they passive? Are they argumentative, defensive, or dismissive? Are you mostly talking or listening, or are you able to devote adequate time and attention to both?

Listening actively rather than passively not only makes people feel respected, but it has huge benefits for your wellbeing as well as those of your relationships. Studies suggest that pleasant social interactions offer better life satisfaction and a sense of belonging.[43] It also helps build better connections and can help reduce the gap between intended and actual outcomes.

Julian Treasure developed a simple way of remembering the key steps for active listening through the acronym RASA:[44] **Receive** - Give the person time to say what they need to. **Appreciate** - Offer noticeable gestures and noises (Ummm, yes, I see, etc.), so the other person is aware of your attention. **Summarize** - Recount back to them or paraphrase what they have just said. **Ask** - Ask lots of questions to get a better understanding and clarify the meaning behind what they said.

Today we ask the question, how can you bring more awareness to your conversations? How can you start to recognize what is not being said as much as what is being said? The exercise on day 16 challenges you to resist the urge to jump in and offer your thoughts, opinion, or solution until someone has completed what they are trying to say.

This is such a great activity that can be used on family, friends, children, work colleagues, or pretty much anyone you meet today. If you find that this day falls at a time when you have limited opportunities to converse with others, you can swap this activity for another day and come back to it.

Challenge yourself to actively listen for the entire day.

TASK 16

Truly listen to everyone you meet today and resist ALL urges to interrupt, even if you find the conversation extremely boring or emotive!!

Authentically demonstrate visible cues that you are listening, such as nodding, smiling, and acknowledging (Ummm, yes, I see, etc.). Watch for those non-verbal cues (what is not being said). You can also paraphrase or summarize what you heard.

Ask questions and be curious (this is particularly good with children). Watch closely what happens to someone's face when you actively listen.

For an informative read, check out: I Hear You: The Surprisingly Simple Skill Behind Extraordinary Relationships *by Michael S. Sorensen* ☺

Intentional Listening - Reflection

On day 16, the exercise was to simply listen. Easy, right? Did you notice any difference between hearing and listening? What happened? How did you find applying the active listening activity to different people? Did you attract any different responses than usual?

Resisting the urge to interrupt or "help the conversation along" may be challenging for some, especially when you are busy. Picking up on the earlier awareness exercises, you may wish to reflect on what thoughts and feelings were present at the time of your listening. Did you have lots of inner dialogue going on throughout the conversation, or did you make a real conscious effort to avoid offering your opinion, even when you felt your input was valid? If one of your conversations was in a work context, what did this feel like in comparison to a social setting? Was it beneficial, or did it hinder the conversation?

Remember, when you actively listen and positively engage in a conversation, you can start to hear what is not being said as much as what is being said. When people really feel listened to, they feel heard. It is not only wonderful for building and maintaining relationships, but it is much more time-efficient too!

Next steps

You have two options:

1. For the rest of this week, make a point of actively listening to every conversation you have. Observe what effect the power of listening has on each person you speak to. Notice whether they are listening to you. How might you further influence this?

2. Write a few observational notes on what you discovered and move on to Day 17 with a new focus.

Whatever you decide, it is your journey towards extending your power of influence.

TAKE NOTE

DAY 17

Mindful Speaking

"The way you speak to others can offer them joy, happiness, self-confidence, hope, trust, and enlightenment. Mindful speaking is a deep practice."

– THICH NHAT HANH

Mindful Speaking

Every time you speak, is it with full awareness? Following on from yesterday's activity, where you practiced the art of active listening, today's activity complements this exercise by helping you increase your awareness of how you speak to people. Most people may feel pretty good about the way in which they speak to others, but what happens if you are challenged by a stressful situation, if you meet someone you really don't want to speak with, or if you are in a mega rush? Mindful speaking can considerably reduce episodes of miscommunication, build strong relationships, and create a more effective workforce.[45]

Consider this scenario: You find yourself in a situation that you have been in many times before when you meet a colleague, family member, or acquaintance, and they start a conversation that you don't really want to hear. Do you a) start speaking over them to change the topic, b) cut them off right away and share that you are either too "busy" to talk, or more bluntly, tell them you don't want to hear this, or c) try and understand why they have raised this same topic again and use your words wisely to draw out their concerns/excitements/thoughts?

If you chose "c", congratulations for exercising great patience and awareness. If, however, you chose "a" or "b" and fit with the great majority of society, today's activity will be perfect for you. Those of you who are fortunate enough to have lots of friends, family, and/or work colleagues/customers may have access to hundreds of conversations every day. It could be that you converse with the same person or with lots of different people, either face-to-face, over the phone, or online. Today's activity will explore the intent and awareness behind those words you use.

If you have heard the phrase "speaking without thinking", this is a lot more common than you may realize. Humans are often wrapped up in a cycle of responding to conversations without full awareness of how their message is coming across. They react to others automatically, heavily influenced by their personal lens, the environment they are in, their inner dialogue, along with any previous conversations and interactions they have had with that person.

You will no doubt recognize the value of using kind words when communicating but being aware of your natural tendencies when speaking with different individuals, especially during times of emotional pressure, will enable you to influence all those you come into contact with, in a positive way. It can make or break down relationships, both at work and in the home environment, and it can have huge benefits to your mental health and those around you.[46]

With mindful speaking, you get to choose the words or the feelings you wish to share rather than your words ruling you. It is also crucial to adapt your conversation and tone throughout, depending on the non-verbal cues that you are receiving. If you have ever experienced a situation when you have said something that you wish you hadn't or have upset someone unintentionally, this will be your words controlling you! How we "show up" in a conversation is important, so consider whether you speak to everyone you meet in the same way. If you find yourself speaking to a friend, a colleague, or the cashier in the local shop differently, why is this? What is your intention behind each interaction? Are any specific interactions you have more "important" than the others? What is your body language saying? What words do you choose to use, or do you just 'freestyle' it? How authentic in your response are you?

Evidence suggests that people are pretty good liars when it comes to sharing how they really feel.[47] Have you ever said you were fine when you were not? Or maybe you said "okay" when asked to do something you really didn't want to do? Learning these patterns of behavior will help you understand where you might wish to change. Then allow yourself to feel a pause before you speak, and choose your words wisely.

TASK 17

Speak to someone differently today. Continuing to use your skills learned from the active listening activity on day 16, go into this conversation with the intention of making them feel good.

Observe closely what is happening behind the words you and they speak. Notice them and the value of their words without judgment.

Before you respond, pause, and purposefully choose words that will promote a positive response, both in you and in this person. Notice any emotions that arise.

For an expressive read, check out: The Five Keys to Mindful Communication by Susan Gillis Chapman 😊

Speaking Mindfully - Reflection

When you begin a conversation, particularly if this is within a work or activity context, you may find that you are led by an objective you wish to achieve. This objective will have an impact on your inner dialogue which can reflect in how you speak. Sometimes, by changing your objective, for example, from: "I need information from this person" to "I am curious what this person thinks", you can change the manner in which you speak to them.

What effect did having a positive agenda have on your conversation on day 17? How did it differ from how you normally approach communication? Did focusing on how you wanted the person to feel, rather than the task you wished to achieve, change the course of the conversation? If so, what happened?

By introducing silences or pauses before you speak, you are demonstrating empathy and self-enquiry.[48] Did you notice anything happening in your body when you paused before responding? Did it feel good? Was it too long? Odd? Uncomfortable? Write some notes on your experiences. You may also wish to take this exercise to the next level and mirror or mimic (subtly!) the other person you are speaking to.[49]

Next steps   .

You have two options:

1. Continue to try out this exercise on the different types of relationships you have for the remainder of the week. Start to mirror or mimic the gestures of the other person - you may find that this happens naturally if you are both fully engaged in the conversation. Write down any observations you make.

2. Write a few observational notes on what you discovered and move on to Day 18 with a new focus.

Whatever you decide, it is your journey towards extending your power of influence.

TAKE NOTE

DAY 18

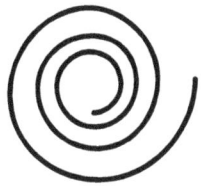

Positive Influencing

*"Our minds influence the key
activity of the brain, which then
influences everything; perception,
cognition, thoughts and feelings,
personal relationships; they're all a
projection of you."*

– DEEPAK CHOPRA

Positive Influencing

Is the old adage "you can't change other people" true?
In life, you will no doubt come across people with whom
you feel conflicted. It could be that they don't share the
same values as you, perhaps they appear dismissive or
cold, or you may get a feeling that they don't like you
for whatever reason.

Today, the question is: Can you change other people
or at least influence how they behave around you?
Maybe you cannot physically change other people,
even if you might want to, but you can change the way
you think, feel, and behave towards them. The exercise
on day 18 will introduce you to a technique that can
disrupt subconscious patterns of irritation, disdain, or
disconnect that you might experience when you come
across any person that you simply "don't like!". You will
start by identifying a person that you feel conflicted or
challenged by and start to consider all the positive things
about them. Similarly to how you became aware of and
changed the narrative about yourself earlier in this book,
now is the time to put this into practice with others.

Conflicts in relationships can cause significant stress,
which can manifest itself in poor physical and mental
health, extreme or low levels of anxiety, and increased
tension at home and at work.[50] There is even some
research on conflicted couples that suggests that when

one partner repetitively suppresses anger throughout the relationship, they may both die younger. [51] Wow!

Rather than suppressing, ignoring, or even trying to remove the conflict, the approach will be centered around you changing your perception of other people. Despite often feeling uncomfortable, it is good to remember that some conflicts are necessary for growth and development, and which may enable you to see another person's view.[52] You don't have to always agree with everyone, but you can choose the way you behave reactively with certain people, which can lead to a quicker resolution.

To prepare you for this next exercise, can you recognize any patterns of behavior that might arise when communicating with different individuals? Think of a person whose company you greatly enjoy. What are the characteristics that make this relationship particularly good? How does this differ from someone who you find it hard to connect with?

When you come across people who repetitively challenge you, it is not uncommon to develop a set of automated responses, sometimes triggering a fight, flight, or freeze reaction. Your body sees this person as a threat and releases adrenalin and cortisol to get you ready for conflict. Try and become aware, the next time you see that person, of what reaction you have.

Can you notice any difference in your body, your head, your behavior, or all three? When you get this type of involuntary reaction, most of your responses come from the emotional brain, which is poised and ready to deal with any danger. This links back to the lesson from day three, which illustrated how your feelings and emotions could greatly impact your behavior, leading you to potentially approach each conversation with this person or persons through the lens of previous interactions, automatically starting you off on the wrong foot, so to speak.

To break the habit, it is important to break any cycles of rumination where you go into a spiral of irritation and anguish every time you think of them. In today's exercise, you will be guided to spend some time embracing the positive attributes this person has, no matter how hard it may be for you to see! It could be anything positive, such as their strengths, values, virtues, or even something physical about them. For example, do you like the way they dress, style their hair, or their taste in music? Consider their vulnerabilities and their fears, their interests, and their connections. Try and separate the person from their behaviors and dig deeper, as the benefits will be worth it in the long run.

TASK 18

In your notebook, call to mind a person who you feel challenged by, and write their name at the top of the page. Now, create two columns and write on the left ten positive things about this person.

Read the list out loud and in the right column, write down any positive feelings you have as a result of reading the first list. For example, "I feel grateful and respected when they are 'always on time' for me".

End with a gentle smile, saying to yourself, "I am willing to love and accept [say name here]". If you discover that your inner critic is being very vocal, take a deep breath, stick with it, and keep repeating the phrase.

For the best ever read, check out: How to Win Friends and Influence People *by Dale Carnegie* ☺

Positive Projection - Reflection

How did it feel to do this exercise? Did you notice any emotions, both positive and negative, during the process? What was your inner dialogue saying? Did it agree with the positive things you were writing, or was it shouting at you with all the bad stuff they do? If the latter, were you able to overcome the distractions and maintain your focus on the positive?

While this activity only requires a short time in one day to create the list and contemplate the good things about this challenging person, the change of mindset towards them may take a little longer. Now that your list is complete, you may wish to use visualization to see yourself meeting this person and having a positive and friendly interaction with them.

Refer to your list often to remind yourself of the positive attributes of this individual, particularly if you have encountered another challenging interaction with them. When you next come into contact with this person, first compliment them on something positive to disrupt any automated negative patterns and connect with their positive attributes. After a while, they may very well change how they interact with you.

Next steps

You have two options:

1. Repeat this exercise daily, reconfirming all the positive things about this person and visualizing positive interactions with them before you meet next with them.

2. Write a few observational notes on what you discovered and move on to Day 19 with a new focus.

Whatever you decide, it is your journey towards extending your power of influence.

TAKE NOTE

DAY 19

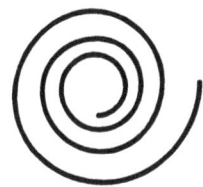

Random Acts of Kindness

"How do we change the world?
One random act of kindness
at a time."

– MORGAN FREEMAN

Random Acts of Kindness

What have you done for another person today? You may already have heard about the topic for today's activity, but were you aware that performing random acts of kindness for someone else can actually impact the health of your heart and even increase your life span?[53] Studies have shown that regular practice of kindness can increase your happiness in just one week, making it one of the quickest ways to boost your long-term wellbeing.[54] It has also been used as part of a treatment plan for those experiencing depression and anxiety. Being kind to others is not only hugely beneficial to your health, emotional wellbeing, and general happiness, it is simply a wonderful thing to do for another human being.

With the increase of technology, the gap in socialization resulting from the pandemic, and society becoming more physically disconnected, this may be one of the most important activities you can do, not only for your own wellbeing but for the wider world. If you are the type of person who already regularly likes to 'give', take some time to consider what more you can do. Perhaps you are a person who is already aware of the benefits of practicing acts of kindness, but there is an expectation of something in return. For example, you let someone out in traffic, and when they don't wave or mime thank you, you get annoyed with them.

The task today is about unconditional random acts of kindness without expecting anything in return—no smiles, no thank yous, nothing, except knowing you did something good for another person. Sometimes people can get so caught up in reacting to their lives subconsciously that they may be blind at that moment to your generosity, but be reassured that it will have impacted them positively in some way, even if you never discover how.

It is equally crucial that you are open and able to accept kindness and gratitude in return. If you are the type of person who retorts with "Ah, it was nothing" or "Really, it's no big deal!" then stop! Accept each moment of gratitude with graciousness and feel the full appreciation with an open heart. This part of the process cannot be underestimated!

The concept "Pay it Forward" was first documented by Lily Hardy Hammond in her 1916 novel In the Garden of Delight, but was popularized in 2000 by the Kevin Spacey and Helen Hunt movie of the same name, where a schoolteacher tells his class to take the things they don't like about the world and flip it upside down, by helping three other people, asking for nothing in return. Most recipients pay the kindness forward.

In 2002, a customer in a drive-through coffee shop in Winnipeg, USA, chose to pay for the order of the car behind her. This small act of kindness was so gratefully received that they paid the bill for the car behind them.[55] This generosity chain went on for three hours, enjoyed by 226 customers! Consider, then, how just one act of kindness can have a spiral effect on society and the greater world. However, today we will start a little bit smaller and start with self. To make a difference, you need to be aware—aware of yourself and aware of those around you.

Kindness brings communities together, strengthens relationships, and gives people hope and optimism. On day 19 of your 28 days of positivity, take this opportunity to see what effect you can have on those close to you and further afield. Find your power of influence through kindness and bring it everywhere you go today and in everything you do.

You can find a list of ideas to get you inspired on: www.zeenahicks.com/28days-positivity

TASK 19

Today, have fun performing random acts of kindness.

This could include complimenting each person you meet today, buying someone you don't know a coffee, bringing flowers to someone you care about, or offering to do something for someone you don't normally do.

Look out for things that you can do that might bring a little bit of joy to another person and evoke an unconditional feeling of kindness. Make sure that you also keep yourself open to receiving kindness and enjoy the experience of both giving and receiving.

For a heartfelt read, check out: Random Acts of Kindness: How to Make It a Better World *by The Editors of Conari Press* 🙂

Random Acts of Kindness - Reflection

How did it feel to offer unconditional acts of kindness in today's activity? Use the notes in this book or in your journal to evaluate all of the thoughts, feelings, and emotions that came up for you.

Did you find yourself expecting any outcome along the way? If so, this is not uncommon, as giving and receiving are often perceived as one and the same. Were there any surprising outcomes that you weren't expecting? Did you find yourself experiencing an emotional recall following the experience? For example, did you play back the great feeling in your mind? These are all really positive outcomes for your first experience.

The Random Acts of Kindness Foundation has a number of great resources, tools, and ideas on its website that can inspire you further if you wish to dive deeper. They also offer an opportunity to become a RAKTIVIST—an ambassador for kindness in your organization or community. Their mantra is #makekindnessthenorm. [56]

Next steps

You have two options:

1. Try and carry out one random act of kindness every day for a week without expecting anything in return. Be creative and think big. Mix it up a bit by engaging with people you know and complete strangers. Document how you feel after each event and at the end of the week.

2. Write a few observational notes on what you discovered and move on to Day 20 with a new focus.

Whatever you decide, it is your journey towards extending your power of influence.

TAKE NOTE

DAY 20

Letter of Appreciation

"If all you did was look for things to appreciate, you would live a joyous, spectacular life."

– ABRAHAM-HICKS

Letter of Appreciation

Who would you like to thank? If you have read this book so far in order, you may have noticed that positive psychology is more than just looking at things from a positive perspective or thinking positively. It is a multifaceted approach, which is wholly appropriate given that humans are multifaceted beings. There is no one way to arrive at positivity. It is a practice and way of being that is enjoyed, challenged, and nurtured on a daily basis, and it is not only just about you.

How you show up in the world and how you interact with others is as important as having a "zen" mind. Can you recall anyone in your life that had a positive impact on you? It could be a teacher, a friend, a family member, a work colleague, or a random stranger whom you have never seen again. What was the situation? What did they do? What was it about this person that impacted you the way it did? What were your thoughts and feelings at the time? How did these thoughts and feelings impact your behavior? Can you list all the positive things that made this person unique in their approach to you?

If you have never asked these questions before, you may want to reflect on whether you shared your appreciation with this person at the time, or maybe the impact wasn't apparent until after a longer period.

Use the notes section to capture your reflection. Often, life takes you on a journey only to discover you missed some moments, which either didn't make sense at the time or you were too preoccupied to notice what was in front of you. With this in mind and expanding on the gratitude exercise on day nine, today's activity centers around sharing your appreciation in a letter to someone who you feel has positively impacted your life. Whether or not they are aware of how they impacted you, now is your time to say thank you.

Appreciation is one of those emotions that, when experienced, can minimize and even eradicate feelings of sadness, remorse, or disappointment. This exercise combines a number of positive psychology concepts, including reflective writing, gratitude, and savoring. The science behind this activity is similar to that of the gratitude exercise in that it has been shown to increase happiness and wellbeing.[57] It also has a positive impact on your relationships, and not only with the person you send the letter to.[58]

Today's exercise allows you to feel the full benefits of embodying gratitude, as well as strengthen connections and relationship bonds. It is also simply a wonderful thing to do for another person and passes on positivity to others. So, today, you are invited to write a letter to an individual who supported you through a challenging time or gave you something, emotionally or physically, that has influenced you positively today. The person may or may not be aware of this metaphorical gift that they gave you, and it is likely you haven't ever expressed your full heartfelt appreciation to them. Today is your opportunity to do this.

Use the time during the activity to savor the appreciation that you have for the person you choose to write to. Try and avoid any temptation to rush, taking the opportunity to reflect and fully embrace any emotions that arise when you consider their intentions towards you. In this exercise, don't be afraid to open yourself up and be vulnerable, as in, it is okay to feel uncomfortable doing this! Depending on the circumstances, the situation, and the person, each individual might approach this in a very different way, and that is okay. Remember, this is your journey, and simply doing the process of writing and feeling appreciation is a great start.

Should you need help writing this letter, there are some tips on: www.zeenahicks.com/28days-positivity

TASK 20

Write a letter of appreciation to someone you know. Tell them in detail what they did, which meant so much to you. Share how this impacted you at the time and thereafter. End the letter by stating how grateful you are to them. Be open, be honest, and be vulnerable.

If possible, hand deliver the letter, and ask them to read it in front of you. Watch for opportunities to savor the experience and further strengthen the bond between you.

If hand delivering is completely impractical, you may wish to email the letter, read it out over the phone, or share it with this person over a video call.

For a gratifying read, check out: A Simple Act of Gratitude: How Learning to Say Thank You Changed My Life *by John Kralik* ☺

Letter of Appreciation - Reflection

While writing a letter of appreciation is a great gift for another person, you may have noticed a number of benefits for yourself with this activity. Can you recall the feelings that you experienced as you were thinking back as to why this person made such an impact on you?

Did you notice any emotional reaction in your body as you reflected on the experience? If so, can you relate this feeling to joy, happiness, love, hope, or empowerment? See if you can recall any of these emotions again as you think about what you wrote.

Did you hand deliver or send the letter another way? When you hand over this type of letter and suggest they read it in front of you, you may be privileged to see their most authentic response. If you delivered the letter by hand or another way, what reaction did you get from the person you wrote to? How might you describe their reaction, and how did that feel? If you experienced emotion, was it a different feeling than what you experienced when writing the letter? Did this experience have any impact on your current or potential future relationship with this person?

Next steps

You have two options:

1. If this felt good, consider writing a letter of appreciation once a week, or month, to each of the people who have made an impact on your life. If you are no longer in contact with that person, you may still wish to write the letter and store it should you ever meet again.

2. Write a few observational notes on what you discovered and move on to Day 21 with a new focus.

Whatever you decide, it is your journey towards extending your power of influence.

TAKE NOTE

DAY 21

Compassion

"If you want others to be happy, practice compassion. If you want to be happy, practice compassion."

– DALAI LAMA

Compassion

How compassionate are you? Compassion and positive psychology go hand in hand. It is the glue that holds society together, the thread that stitches relationships back together, and the force that drives individuals to pick themselves up and move forward. It gives the world balance and connects us with our truth. The practice of compassion involves awareness, empathy, and visible interest. It is the ability to put oneself in another's shoes; it's a two-way street, and the rewards can be mutually felt.

Almost everyone, if not all, who reads this book may understand what it means to be compassionate to another person. You might share compassion with family members or friends without thinking when they are going through a difficult time or need a little extra support. Unfortunately, though, people are not always that great at displaying the same level of compassion towards themselves. For example, think of a time when you feel you made a pretty big mistake. Consider what level of compassion you experienced from yourself. It is highly likely that it was very little, or perhaps there was none. You may have played the error over and over again in your head and repetitively verbally abused yourself. Now, consider if your best friend, partner, or child made a mammoth mistake. Would you treat them the same way? Most probably not!

Compassion is about recognizing and appreciating the suffering someone may be going through rather than making it worse, brushing it off, or ignoring the experience. When you practice self-compassion, you are acknowledging, without judgment, that what you are going through may feel difficult and hard to deal with, but that's okay. You may also consider that all humans make mistakes and experience challenging times, just like you. Then, in the same way, you might treat a friend or family member that requires a little TLC (tender loving care), you would be kind to yourself, offer reassuring words, and recognize that this will pass.

Here is an example in action. The next time you make a mistake that affects you emotionally, rather than give in to the temptation to call yourself an array of negative insults, you might recognize the horrible feeling you have inside, with your stomach churning, heavy heart, and the feeling of blood rushing from your head. Once you fully appreciate the response you are having, you could let yourself know that this is a completely normal reaction, and instead of making things a lot worse for yourself, you could consider all the things that might make you feel better. By practicing self-compassion, you are allowing yourself to fully experience a natural cycle of emotions, which is a healthier approach for your mental health and wellbeing.

The body of research is growing, with studies linking self-compassion to less anxiety and lower risks of depression; reduced burn-out amongst medical professionals; improved parent-child relationships; better job satisfaction; and if that's not enough, you can even age more positively![59] Practicing compassion and displaying empathy for others can improve relationships, build trust, improve collaboration, and enhance loyalty.[60] The tide is shifting in the workplace too, with compassionate leadership being used more frequently in large and small businesses, with compassionate leaders being perceived as more competent and stronger.[61]

Today's exercise draws from Kristen Neff's work on self-compassion, which connects you with your "non-ego" self, letting go of perfection or perceived inadequacy to encourage greater emotional resilience.[62] You are invited to sit with any discomfort, stress, or worry and find the strength within to experience and nurture self-compassion. If you get stuck, think kindness, and not pity, so rather than ignoring or wallowing in the feelings that arise for you, lean into them, feel them, and accept what comes up, knowing you are not alone and are safe in the space.

TASK 21

Identify an area of stress or worry in your life (nothing too overwhelming). Close your eyes and sit with this feeling. Rather than focusing on the worst possible outcome, appreciate every thought, feeling, and impact that this worry or stress has on you.

In your mind, see another person who may share a similar worry or experience. You don't have to know them; just be aware that this probability exists somewhere. Finding compassion and kindness in your heart, reach out to them metaphorically and let them know it is going to be okay; that this will pass and you are here for them.

Now direct these same intentions towards yourself. Place your hand on your heart while doing this if it feels good.

For a sincere read, check out: Radical Compassion: Learning to Love Yourself and Your World with the Practice of RAIN *by Tara Brach* ☺

Self Compassion - Reflection

How did it feel to sit with your emotions throughout this exercise? How long did your emotions last? Neuroscience indicates that the body's chemical reaction to most emotional responses lasts less than 90 seconds.[63] This means any hurt, upset, shock, fear, anger, or worry you feel will only evoke a physiological response for less than a minute and a half. If you feel it for longer than this time, there's a possibility that you are choosing to stay in an emotional loop, albeit subconsciously.

By sitting with your feelings, you can ride out the wave of emotion and accept it as part of your natural physicality. Watch out for any inner narrative that might be keeping you in a loop.

You can also help others when they get emotional by reassuring them and distracting them. Once 90 seconds have passed, you can start to encourage them through their natural chemical and emotional response, guiding them away from any cycles of perpetuating thoughts related to the emotional upset.

A guided self-compassion meditation can be found on: www.zeenahicks.com/28days-positivity

Next steps

You have two options:

1. Exercise compassion with yourself or another person in real time when a problem occurs. Take some deep breaths and stay present while you notice the 90-second rule. Write down your observations.

2. Write a few observational notes on what you discovered and move on to Day 22 with a new focus.

Whatever you decide, it is your journey towards extending your power of influence.

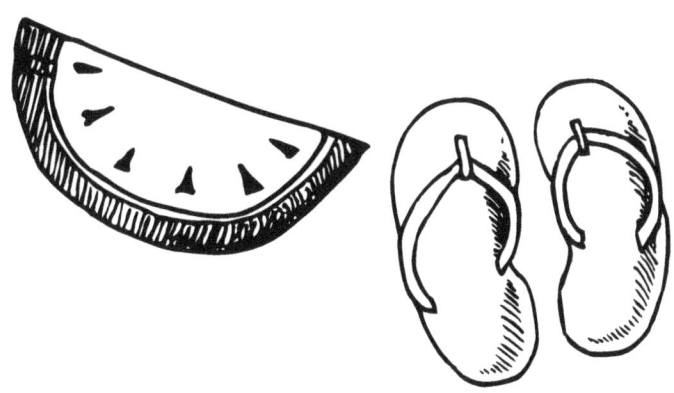

TAKE NOTE

WEEK THREE REFLECTIONS

Use this section to recap on the past week

What resonated with you the most this week?

Which exercise did you find most challenging in week three and why?

How can you close the gap between where you are and where you want to be?

Further Reflections:

WEEK FOUR –
TIME TO TAKE ACTION

f you have managed to do each of the activities in this book so far, huge congratulations on your commitment to self-development and personal growth. By now, you will have broadened your awareness of any patterns and behaviors that may be holding you back. You will also have discovered some concepts and tools to alter your emotional state and mood to a more positive position and learned a little bit about how to become more intentional with other people, which can impact your and others' emotional wellbeing.

The final week in this book will demonstrate your power of influence and set a plan in motion to make things happen! Essentially, this is where you become the master of your own life. In week four, you will choose who, what, and where you want to be and start taking the first steps towards achieving your vision and goals. You will gain a clear understanding of who you are, what you want, and how to motivate yourself to realize it all.

As you enter this week, take a moment to fully appreciate all you have achieved so far. Reflect on which exercises particularly resonated with you and ask yourself why you feel you connected with them most. What do you feel was the outcome of doing the activities? Did anything shift for you?

In week three, you will have played with the influence you have on yourself and others by making small steps to be more aware through positive intention. Week four continues this work, and you will start to uncover your power of influence on future personal outcomes.

Consider for a moment that you've come across a beautifully crafted old oak wooden door with a big shiny key in it. You turn the key easily and open the door. Behind the door is you, living your happiest life yet. What year is it? What are you doing? Who are you with? How is it different from now? This week you will further expand that image, and you will start to pro-actively create this life rather than accepting limitations and settling for a reactive you. It is time to get creative!

Resist any urge to put this book down now. If you start to feel this is too much work, try and figure out why you have this response. Is the life you want too much effort, or are you ready to build it and realize it? Now is the time to become the architect of your own life. If you feel challenged by any of this, recognize that this is a natural response to change. If you feel comfortable doing any of the exercises, push yourself to go deeper. Allow yourself to feel inspired, elated, and excited, but equally embrace any feelings of frustration, fear, or uncertainty, knowing that the work you put in to navigate through these feelings will yield huge dividends in the long term.

DAY 22

Authenticity

"This above all;
to thine own self be true."

– WILLIAM SHAKESPEARE, HAMLET

Authenticity

Who am I? It is that burning question that many people ask themselves and often never find the answer. Well, today is going to be different. Today you are going to explore what it means to be You. To be your true and authentic self.

Authenticity is one of those buzzwords that have been popularized over the last decade as people try to find meaning and "fit in" (or not) with the rest of the world. Society is built around creating parameters for people to fit into. We experience this very early on when we are assigned a gender and name at birth. It is reflected in our cultures, religions, and spirituality. Family, education, peers, and life experiences shape our understanding of the world and help form our personalities. What is left is you and a construct of who you believe you are—your values, your dreams, and your desires. But who are you really? What does it mean to be your authentic self? And why do people struggle so much with it?

Research has revealed that those who live more authentically have better relationships, higher self-esteem, lower anxiety and stress, and generally experience more positivity and happiness.[64] It might be that being true to yourself and standing up for what you believe in didn't work out for you in the past, and as a result, you may hide behind your true feelings to protect yourself or others. For some, the fear of rejection, or the potential for others to not fully support you, may be enough to keep the true you from appearing. You then end up becoming a puppet for the amalgamation of external programming that you have picked up or had forced upon you over the years, serving others and not yourself.

There is always hope, though. Imagine, for just a moment, living out of this world on another planet, and coming down from space to earth for the very first time. Landing wherever you liked, what would most resonate with you? What aspects of Earth do you think you might like? Using your five senses of sight, scent, taste, touch, and sound, try to connect with those things, people, and places that bring you the most joy. Now ask yourself, "Why do I like this?" There may also be things that you don't connect with, that you don't necessarily like. Again, using your senses, ask yourself why you do not like this. The key aspect of this process is trying to disconnect from any potential emotional influence you may be drawing from previous experiences, connections with people, or things you have previously learned. Moving away from preconceptions and past learnings, this disconnection and reconnection might help you start to become closer to your authentic self.

If you ever find yourself not saying what you really feel, with fear that you will upset, irritate, or negatively influence another person's opinion of you. Or maybe you end up doing things that you really don't want to do. These behaviors will conflict with your authentic self, and the results will unknowingly affect your mental health and wellbeing. Building on week one, recognizing where you are conflicted, may be the first step towards living a true, meaningful life. It is obviously not going to happen in just one day, but today's exercise aims to give you a flavor of what it might be like to move away from natural bias and lean more into your authentic self.

Today you will be guided to explore in more depth those things that you actually like, that represent the real you. Authenticity enables you to live your life according to your own personal values and strengths without being influenced by other people and outside forces. Sounds simple, right? It is, but it is not necessarily easy. Today you will play with letting go of who you are "supposed" to be or who people want you to be. It is about leaning into who you "feel" you are when you remove all the external influences that keep you stuck. It is about believing, whoever you are, that "you are enough".

In the words of the wonderful Bréne Brown, it is time to let go of who you think you are supposed to be and embrace who you are![65]

TASK 22

On a page, create two columns, and in one, write down all of the things that really make you feel energized, invigorated, excited, and powerful. This is your "love it" list.

Call the second column your "bin it" list, and write down all of the things that really demotivate, frustrate, or make you angry. These are the things that conflict with your true self.

Looking at the list, take some deep breaths, and on the out-breath, cross out each of the things on the 'bin it' list that are out of your control, releasing them as you go. For the rest of the day, focus primarily on your energizing list, incorporating as many of them as you can in your day.

For a genuine read, check out: Authentic: How to be yourself and why it matters *by Stephen Joseph* ☺

Love it List - Reflection

Look at both lists you created and reflect on what you wrote. Were the lists balanced, or did one appear to outweigh the other? As this exercise appears in week four, hopefully, you will have found lots of things on the "love it" list and fewer on the "bin it" list! If your "bin it" list was rather lengthy, how much of it did you identify that was out of your control?

The fun bit is releasing those things that don't serve you and shifting focus towards those things that are closer to your values and a sense of purpose. Living authentically encourages you to find the balance between the goodness that is inside you and how you translate this into the things you do and say in the outside world. It will require you to accept your vulnerability and put aside any defense mechanisms you may have stored up from childhood and other later life experiences.

The next few exercises this week will help you formulate a plan to move forward towards living more authentically and start outlining what you want in life rather than what is being served up to you. Now is your time to take intentional positive action to be the change you wish to see.

Next steps

You have two options:

1. Over the next week, notice where you find yourself not being authentic and make a note of what happened and why you felt disconnected from yourself. Consider what you could do differently next time, and then find three things to do on your "love it" list to reconnect with the real you.

2. Write a few observational notes on what you discovered and move on to Day 23 with a new focus.

Whatever you decide, it is your journey towards creating the life you want.

TAKE NOTE

DAY 23

Purpose and Meaning

"Life is never made unbearable
by circumstances, but only by
lack of meaning and purpose."

– VICTOR FRANKL

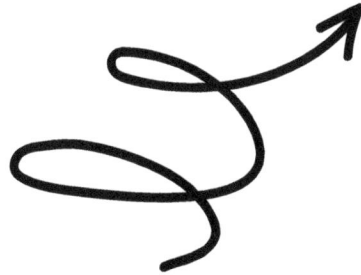

Purpose and Meaning

Have you ever thought about your purpose in life? That might sound like a big question, but it is not uncommon for people to reflect back on moments and events in their life and ask, "WHY?" If you have never contemplated this, well, you have a treat in store, as today's activity explores what having a purpose means and if, in fact, you really need one.

According to research, you are likely to lead a longer, happier, and even wealthier life if you have a purpose.[66] But, if that is not enough to inspire you, purpose can be understood as the reason you get up in the morning and the reason you go to bed at night. It is responsible for the meaning that life brings to you and the journey you take in life. It is the motivation behind the goals you have, no matter how small; it is the reason why you exist.

If you have ever said to yourself, "What am I doing this for?" or "What is the point of this?" or "There must be more than this", then that is you searching for more meaning in your life and endeavoring to find your purpose. Now, this doesn't necessarily mean that everyone was born for a higher purpose, but it does suggest that humans seek to be valued and significant to someone, something, or someplace. For some people, this will be instinctive and natural to find, but for others, it may be a continual journey of discovery, trial, and change.

If you think back to your childhood when you had aspirations and visions of the future, what was it you wanted to do? Where did you want to go and see? Who did you want to be with or spend your time with? Thinking about where you are right now, how many of the things you aspired to do as a child have you achieved or are still at the forefront of your mind? If the answer is none, why not? What has changed, and are you happy with that change? At what point did you realize these visions? Or did they become just dreams?

Sometimes a person's purpose might appear in the most unlikely situations, and occasionally it might be the margin between life and death. You may hear stories of extraordinary feats of survival against all odds. Often, these survivors, when asked how they made it through, have one common theme: The focus on something more than self. A will to survive for someone or something else; for something yet to be accomplished; or an unwavering hope that there is more to be part of.

In Victor Frankl's heart-rending recount of his experiences in Auschwitz, "A Man's Search for Meaning", he explores how hope, meaning, and purpose became the driving forces for those who overcame immense adversity to survive a harrowing three years in captivity during WWII. The ability to find and hold on to the belief that you are destined for something greater, or at the very least different, beyond any contradictory reality you might be living, could stand in the way of perishing.

On a small island off the coast of Japan, the people of Okinawa are reported to be the happiest people in the world, with many of them living over 100 years of age. This may be down to their healthy lifestyle, strong community, lack of retirement age, or it could be down to a concept called "ikigai".

Ikigai broadly translates to mean the "value of life" and has been equated to living one's life purpose. For the Okinawan community, ikigai is a way of being, maintaining focus on what is good in life, and always reaching out to live the best "you" every day. For some, "ikigai" has been passed on from generation to generation; for others, it is a constantly evolving journey, but each individual owns and drives their value of life, and this appears to be intrinsically linked to their happiness.

The lesson today takes the learnings from this concept and asks you questions for you to contemplate and formulate your 'ikigai' or purpose. Use the worksheet on www.zeenahicks.com/28days-positivity for guidance.

TASK 23

Make four lists answering the following questions: 1. What makes life worth living for me? 2. What do I feel the world needs? 3. What do I enjoy that I can get paid to do? 4. What am I really good at doing?

Don't be aspirational in your approach. Just write what you absolutely believe.

Find the common themes between your answers in these lists: 1 & 4 - This is your passion; 1 & 2 - This is your mission; 2 & 3 - This is your vocation; 3 & 4 - This is your profession.

You can craft your purpose by creating a verb encompassing your passion, mission, vocation, and profession, which you can make into a sentence.

For a purposeful read, check out: The Little Book of Ikigai: The Essential Japanese Way to Finding Your Purpose in Life *by Ken Mogi, Matt Addis, et al.* ☺

Finding Your Ikigai - Reflection

While you were completing the ikigai exercise, did you become aware of any list having more of a significant emotional impact on you? Which list did you feel you most resonated with? Which list felt like a struggle, or where did you feel you had to think a little bit harder?

If you struggled with any of the sections, try to reflect on why this is. Is there anything you can do to free yourself in this area using some of the tools you have learned so far? Be aware that sometimes this activity takes time to do, and that's okay. It might be that you instantly know all the answers, or maybe you fill out some sections, and further insights pop into your head throughout the week.

Don't panic if you don't have all the answers straight away; this doesn't mean you don't have a purpose! It just means that you are still exploring and working things out. This is a great place to be as you will have taken your first steps towards acknowledging that you have much more to offer the world. You can keep coming back to this exercise and see if things shift, change, or refine year-on-year. It is also a great exercise to do for New Year's Eve!

Next steps

You have two options:

1. Once you have identified your purpose, every time you wake up each morning, visualize how you are going to live your purpose that day. To go deeper into this exercise, use the Venn diagram template, which can be found on zeenahicks.com/28days-positivity.

2. Write a few observational notes on what you discovered and move on to Day 24 with a new focus.

Whatever you decide, it is your journey towards creating the life you want.

TAKE NOTE

DAY 24

Best Possible Self

*"A strong, positive self-image
is the best possible preparation
for success."*

– JOYCE BROTHERS

Best Possible Self

Are you living your best possible self? In today's society, many people have incredibly high expectations of themselves and sometimes feel they never quite deliver. Others, however, may not even know what they want and go from day to day in survival mode, reacting to what comes up in the day, being influenced by people around them, the media, and circumstances they feel are out of their control.

The exercise shared today is a widely used positive psychology intervention conceptualized by Professor of Psychological Sciences, Laura A. King, which, broadly speaking, focuses on yourself in the future where everything has worked out awesomely for you, such as your family life, work life, finances, environment, social life, etc., after, of course, you have taken positive action towards it, rather than it appearing like magic! The activity aims to increase optimism and positive expectations and can be used to lift your mood or start formulating your vision and goals for the future[67].

The great thing about this exercise is that YOU choose the outcome. You can decide when you feel like you might be at your best possible point, hopefully not in the too-distant future, and the process enables you to recognize any gaps that you may need to close. The intervention is outlined in three key steps. Firstly, engaging your mind to consider what this future might actually look like. The second step guides you to write freely about a typical day in this fabulous future. Finally, you will be asked to visualize a day as being your best you, engaging all of your senses.

Visualization has been mentioned a few times already throughout this book, but just to clarify, the act of visualizing is to clearly see and connect with something in your mind as if it was real. Kind of daydreaming while you are awake! Engaging your senses is key for any visualization exercise, as this helps trick your brain and body into feeling like you are already experiencing the moment. People visualize most days naturally, but many of you may not realize you are doing it. Unfortunately, humans often visualize the nasty stuff that has happened to them over and over again. It often manifests in that shiver down the spine or raised heartbeat that catches you unaware when you remember an event you don't like. Essentially, you are reliving this moment in your mind's eye, often completely subconsciously. While this might be a little disturbing, it is also great news because it means you are capable of creating an experience just with your mind, and as a result, you can enjoy the feeling of these great benefits.

An easy way to test how great you are at visualizing is to close your eyes and think of a lemon. See the shape of this lemon, with its vibrant yellow color, and imagine feeling the texture. With your eyes still closed, smell the lemon, and imagine cutting into it and tasting the juice. What does it taste like? What are you feeling as a result? If you managed to do this, no matter how fuzzy or vivid the picture, congratulations! You have successfully visualized! Engaging with your senses of sight, touch, smell, and taste also enabled you to trick your brain into thinking this was real. Did you have any facial reactions when you tasted the lemon? Many people do.

There are two kinds of visualization: one engages your senses, as you did with the lemon, and the other has to do with creating a vision of a future point in your life. Today we will use both in tandem, alongside free writing, which we touched upon earlier on in week one.

There has been lots of research on this intervention, from increasing mood, happiness, and general wellbeing following the exercise to longer-term positivity, optimism, and even pain relief.[68] Allow yourself at least 20 minutes to fully immerse yourself in today's task without judging whether anything is possible or not. Just go with it, enjoy whatever comes up, and take time to reflect afterwards.

TASK 24

Set a timer for one minute. Think about yourself one to three years from now, being your best possible self, where things have worked out perfectly.

When one minute is up, set a timer for 10 minutes and write about a typical day as your best possible self in the future. Don't worry about punctuation, grammar, spelling, or repeating yourself.

When the timer finishes, set the timer again for five minutes, close your eyes, and visualize your best self in the future. Engage in the sights, sounds, feelings, smells, and anything else to connect with this moment.

For the best read ever, check out: Learned Optimism: How to Change Your Mind and Your Life Paperback *by Martin E. P Seligman* 😊

Best Possible Self - Reflection

This exercise is one of the lengthier ones in this book, but it is worth making time for as it has lots of great evidence of its efficacy.[69] There are three very distinct parts to this exercise. After you completed it, did you notice any parts of the activity that felt easier or more challenging for you? Did you experience any judgments or limiting beliefs cropping up as you created your best possible future self?

Note down in this book or your journal what felt good and any areas where you think you may not have connected so well. This is a useful thing to do, so when you repeat the activity in the future, you will have a reference point to help you understand any changes.

Having completed the task, were there any key points, achievements, or feelings in your future self that stood out? Were there any surprises? Where are the gaps between where you are now and this vision of the future? Again, write these down as they will become a key component in the goal setting exercise this week.

Next steps

You have two options:

1. Repeat the exercise every three days for the next four weeks, noting down any changes or areas that become more vivid as you work through the weeks. Use it alongside the goal-setting activity and keep track of any themes in the workbook on: www.zeenahicks.com/28days-positivity

2. Write a few observational notes on what you discovered and move on to Day 25 with a new focus.

Whatever you decide, it is your journey towards creating the life you want.

TAKE NOTE

DAY 25

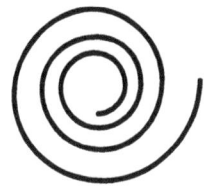

Knowing What You Want

*"The first secret of getting
what you want is knowing
what you want."*

– ARTHUR D. HLAVATY

Knowing What You Want

Do you know exactly what you want in life? If you have been completing this book in sequence, you may by now have a little bit more insight into your purpose and what your best possible self might look like in one to three years. Therefore, you know what you want, right? Don't be disheartened if you are not there yet, as human nature is particularly good at holding on to and focusing on what you don't want.[70] Your natural negativity bias and inner protection mechanism might want to hold you back from where you are most comfortable, so if you find yourself focusing more on where you are now as opposed to where you want to be, read on…

As with the Spice Girls' 1996 song, Wannabe, where the chorus bellows, "I'll tell you what I want, what I really, really want", it is time to get a super clear focus on what you want in every aspect of your life. You have explored previously about the mind not knowing the difference between what is real and what is imagined, so we are about to get creative! If you find yourself either conflicted or distracted throughout the day, it may be that your focus is drifting away from the outcome you believe you want. Knowing and getting what you want can bring you closer to your authentic self, and the work you have done so far will set you up nicely for the remaining tasks in this book.

With so many choices available to people in modern developed societies, it can be challenging to pinpoint exactly what one wants. Then, when you do decide what you want, the compulsion to keep your options open, 'in case it doesn't work out', may very well hold you back or, at the very least, delay you in your journey. The theory of self-determination has been found to be crucial to mental and physical wellbeing in that it gives a person the freedom to make their own choices and decisions without external input.[71] Essentially, it is being given the autonomy to control one's own life, and it can have a huge impact on your motivation to take action, knowing that you can impact the outcome. The only issue is that having so much freedom of choice can delay, undermine, or, at worst, stop you from making any decisions. This is called "choice overload" or the "paradox of choice", which, if not managed, can create overwhelm, anxiety, indecision, and ultimate dissatisfaction.[72]

Knowing what you want is a fundamental step towards living a more positive and happy life. The next step is then to take unwavering action towards those goals. In today's activity, you will refine what you want and become more mindful of those things that you don't want but which may be very present in your life right now. You will focus on five key zones: health and wellbeing; family and/or relationships; business and/or vocation; time freedom; and finances, getting super clear on your desired outcome. You may find that one of two areas in your life might need refined focus, so it is good practice to consider all aspects of your life when assessing where your focus might go. Be aware too of any conflicts between your wants. For example, you may wish to "spend more quality time with my family", but yet your vocational/business want is "to expand my small business to a global franchise". While not impossible, this may be challenging to achieve simultaneously. Putting pressure on yourself to succeed in both areas without appropriate support, may negatively impact your health and wellbeing zone.

As Bill Gates famously said, "we tend to overestimate what we can do in the near future and grossly underestimate what can be done in the distant future," so go wild with your vision for your future. You are the creator of your life, and you can find the strength and determination to believe that you will be able to achieve anything you set your mind to with steadfast passion. Remember that old oak door from the beginning of week four? If you knew that behind it stood everything you ever wanted, would you open it? If not, what's stopping you?

Take your time and use the guide within the workbook on: www.zeenahicks.com/28days-positivity to support you with this next exercise.

TASK 25

Create two columns on a page and label them: 1. Where I am, and 2. Where I want to be.

In the first column, write down the aspects of your current life that you "don't want", but are very present, under the following categories: health and wellbeing; family and/or relationships; business and/or vocation; time freedom; and finances.

In the second column, write down the counter to what you don't want by defining exactly "what you do want".

Once you have created the list, close your eyes, and mentally release those things that you don't want by saying, "I let go of anything that doesn't serve me well, and I welcome… (name the things that you do want)."

For a transcendent read, check out: How to Get What You Want and Want What You Have: A Practical and Spiritual Guide to Personal Success *by John Gray* ☺

Identifying Your Wants - Reflection

If you have been able to define the things that you do want in life, that is a massive step forward! If you are still undecided, simply revisit the activity after a week or two and see if you are further inspired. Did you find any of the categories easier than the others? Was there any category that you felt a little stuck or indecisive in? If this is the case, you may wish to reflect on why this area is presenting a block for you. You may find that talking this through with someone helps.

Were you aware of any negative or restrictive inner dialogue as you completed this exercise, or did you approach it like a child in a sweet shop? What about choice? Were you able to refine it down to exactly what you wanted, or was there any ambiguity in your choices?

Was there any conflict between the categories? Consider carefully how each of your categories connect together. How ambitious are your wants? What would "good" look like for you? Then, ask yourself now, what would "awesome" look like? At this stage, just enjoy creating and building the picture. Day 28 will help you plan how to get there.

Next steps

You have two options:

1. Now that you have your list of where you want to be, close your eyes and, as in the best possible self-exercise, visualize a day in your future life, focusing on what it would feel like to have achieved each of the things on your list.

2. Write a few observational notes on what you discovered and move on to Day 26 with a new focus.

Whatever you decide, it is your journey towards creating the life you want.

TAKE NOTE

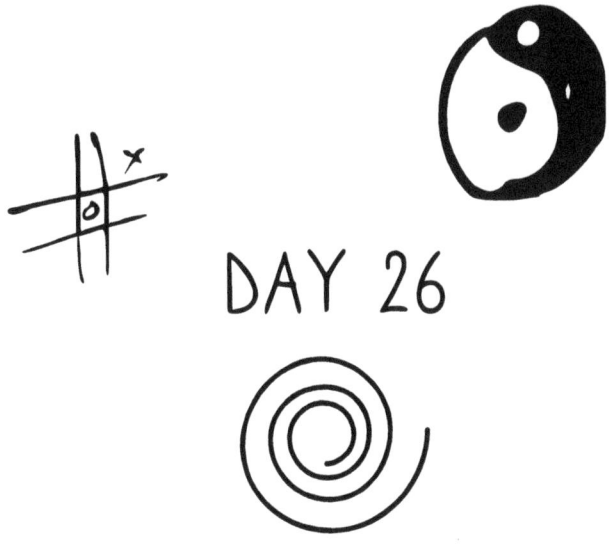

DAY 26

Body Matters

"Our bodies change our minds, and our minds can change our behavior, and our behavior can change our outcomes."

– AMY CUDDY

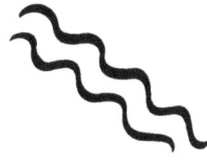

Body Matters

What does your Body Say About You? Hopefully, now that you have decided where you want to be, what it is that you want to realize, and what you want to release, it is time to embody this new you! Today's activity centers around your body and asks the question: Are you in control of your body, or is your body controlling you?

You may have heard the term "body language" before. This is ultimately where your body reflects the thoughts and feelings you have with or without your awareness. For instance, if you taste something that you don't like, it may very well show on your face, such as when you eat something sour if you aren't expecting it. Your body language also says a lot when you are listening (or not listening) to someone, when you are speaking about something emotive, and even when you are thinking quietly to yourself.

Have you ever had someone come up to you and ask, "Are you okay?" yet you thought you had your smiley face on? It could be your body's giving away other signs. During high-pressured situations such as interviews or perhaps in new social circles, your body can say things about you that you may not want to leak out. Your body also responds perfectly well without you when you're dealing with stress and anxiety, so it might be that you find that you've started to experience pain in your back or you're slouching more than normal. Each of these examples is a testament to your being unaware of your body.

To better understand what your body is saying and to build awareness on how you might be able to counteract the effects of unconscious responses, particularly where you experience more stressful or pressured situations, today's activity introduces "Power Posing" as an effective way to own your body and to tap into that inner strength when you notice it flagging at times.

"Power Posing" was popularized by Amy Cuddy, an American social psychologist, who conducted a study demonstrating that people who adopt high power poses can decrease their cortisol levels by 25% and increase their testosterone levels by 19%.[73] Not only that, but it was additionally found that other individuals perceived people who had recently held a power pose to be more confident, influential, and assertive. Power Posing, therefore, appears to be a great way to maintain your focus on your best physical self-objectives, reset your body during times of stress, or when you simply feel you may be lacking a little confidence in your body.

Today's activity explores a couple of poses and positions to encourage you to feel stronger and more confident and perhaps even reduce your stress. This exercise is really useful to do just before interviews, if you're feeling a little down, or if you just want to get a little bit more strength back in your body. The premise is to adopt a position, like Wonder Woman, Superman, or perhaps King Kong, and simply stand like that for two whole minutes. Remember to breathe deeply into the abdomen, breathing regularly and softly, making sure you are breathing through the nose, and notice if that makes a difference.

When you are starting out, you might wish to do this activity behind closed doors, although you could also get the whole family, partners, or friends involved. However, as you approach the exercise, make sure you have fun and enjoy where it takes you. For an emergency booster before an important conversation or meeting, you can find a quiet place to do this activity. Just two minutes can make a big difference!

TASK 26

Adopt a power pose. Think powerful, and stand like a superhero, hands on hips like Wonder Woman or Superman, or stretch your arms out wide like you are trying to offer the world a great big hug!

Monitor the thoughts and feelings you are having. Try and catch any negative or disengaging words in your mind. If you experience limited feelings or words, try and replace the narrative using positive affirmations to evoke a sense of inner and external strength.

Hold this position for at least two minutes and see where it takes you.

For a marvelous read, check out: Presence: Bringing Your Boldest Self to Your Biggest Challenges *by Amy Cuddy* ☺

Power Posing - Reflection

The Power Pose is a wonderful way to connect with your body and own your space. How did you feel when doing your pose? Did you notice what happened to your sternum, the center of your chest, when you took the power pose? As you approach the end of your 28 days, enjoy the renewed energy within your body as you start to take some big action.

Don't worry if you felt completely ridiculous doing the pose. It is as important to observe and note your response following each of these activities. As the exercise aims to bring increased awareness to your body, the more accentuated you make the pose, the more potential for bigger shifts.

You may wish to think about other power poses you could do or consider a power pose you could take into the work environment or meetings. A great tip to keep the power pose feeling, without adopting a full superman pose in a meeting, is to imagine a string has been attached to the center of your chest and you are being pulled upwards to the sky. This automatically lifts your sternum, which can give the impression of confidence and power. Try it for a week and see if it makes a difference.

Next steps

You have two options:

1. In the morning, before you start the day, adopt a power pose, and hold it for two minutes or longer. Add in the words "I am strong" or "I am powerful". Continue doing this daily for one to two weeks and notice if your body language changes. You can also get feedback from someone you know.

2. Write a few observational notes on what you discovered and move on to Day 27 with a new focus.

Whatever you decide, it is your journey towards creating the life you want.

TAKE NOTE

DAY 27

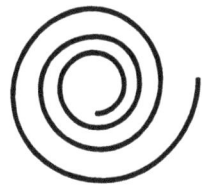

Morning Routine

*"If you win the morning, you
win the day."*

– TIM FERRISS

Morning Routine

How do you start your day? So technically, this is not a positive psychology intervention, but it is an important activity for positivity, general wellbeing, and ultimately making life worth living! Some of the most prolific leaders, celebrities, and influential people in the world have a pro-active morning routine. Having now completed 26 days of positivity activities, your toolbox should now be chock full of interventions that you can choose from to include in your new morning routine.

The first thing to look out for is how you wake up. When you first wake up, do you get up straight away, or are you a bit of a snooze addict? If you tend to hit snooze once or twice, be aware that the simple act of pressing snooze can cause you to lose nearly four hours of productivity time after you wake.[74] This is called sleep inertia, also known as "sleep drunkenness".

Sleep inertia is effectively what happens when you have woken abruptly as your brain transitions between sleeping and waking. It can make you drowsy, get in the way of your morning performance, and reduce your reaction times. It can be very common in new parents, health care practitioners, or military personnel. The simple act of pressing the snooze button can also create sleep drunkenness, as you willingly throw yourself back into a full sleep cycle, only to be rudely awakened by your alarm 10 minutes later. So, the first part of any morning routine is to get up immediately on naturally waking or straight after your alarm goes off, unless you have a spare 90 minutes to take advantage of another full sleep cycle!

In the earlier chapters, you will have explored tools and interventions such as meditation, gratitude exercises, journaling, power posing, laughter yoga, positive affirmations, and savoring. Any or all of these activities work great as part of a morning routine, depending on the time you have set aside. If you are the type of person who leaves the bare minimum amount of time to get up, shower, brush your teeth, dress, and grab a coffee, tea, or other beverage, before running out the door, then you may want to consider resetting your alarm to wake up a bit earlier to fit everything in. Do ensure, however, that you don't cut your sleep to accommodate your earlier wake-up time, keeping in mind that the optimum length for restorative sleep sits between 7-9 hours.[75]

There is tons of research and anecdotal evidence that having a "morning ritual" that you stick to each morning can heavily influence the way you "show up" during the day. Establishing and maintaining a morning routine that helps you focus on consciously approaching the day in the most positive way can give you the perception of more time without rushing;

reduce your stress levels; increase your brain power; protect against mental health and physical illness, such as high blood pressure, diabetes, and heart disease; and increase your energy levels.[76] What's not to love about this?

If you want to take it to the next level, you could even throw in a cold shower, which research suggests is beneficial for both mind and body, strengthening your resilience, giving you a higher state of alertness and focus, increasing your white blood cells, which boosts your immune system, improving your mood, and even helping you lose a bit of weight, if desired.[77] If the very thought of a cold shower fills you with dread, start off with a normal hot shower and turn it cold for the last 30 seconds, and build from there each day. You will notice the difference very soon.

However you decide to seize the day, remember that a morning routine can make the difference in being in control of your day and it controlling you. Draw resources from this book, steal from others, or add your own. Start building slowly or change everything at once. Enjoy creating and discovering a re-energized you! You decide.

TASK 27

In your notebook, write down your current morning routine in list format in a time sequence. Create a column to the right and go down each line in the list and write "keep" or "ditch".

Now create a second list and write down all of the things you would like to do in the morning.

Build your ideal morning routine in your journal or use the workbook notes found on www.zeenahicks.com/28days-positivity to guide you. Then enjoy the process of execution, realizing a new and improved you each day.

For an awakening read, check out: The Miracle Morning: The Not-So-Obvious Secret Guaranteed to Transform Your Life (Before 8 AM) *by Hal Elrod* ☺

Your Morning Routine - Reflection

What did it feel like to create a plan for how you would like to start the morning? What internal dialogue did it bring up for you? Did you find yourself making excuses as to why it wouldn't work, or did you feel excited about the prospect of a more intentional morning?

You may wish to take into account any barriers to your morning success, such as children waking early, late nights, holidays, or unexpected events impacting your morning flow. Try and write down your contingency morning plan for such cases. What could you do instead on these challenging mornings so you don't veer too far off track for too long? You may need to exercise some flexibility, but try and include a strategy for getting back on track the next day.

Consider how your weekend routine differs from your weekday efforts. Try and maintain a level of consistency across the whole week if you can. Don't try to do everything at once and be prepared to adjust your timings as you embed more of your practices, setting your alarm earlier to accommodate this new intentional you!

Next steps

You have two options:

1. Set an intention the night before to wake up at a specific time in the morning and try waking before your alarm goes off. Aim to go to bed early and wake up earlier than you normally would to accommodate three or more positive activities to start your day.

2. Write a few observational notes on what you discovered and move on to Day 28 with a new focus.

Whatever you decide, it is your journey towards creating the life you want.

TAKE NOTE

DAY 28

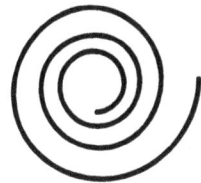

SMART Goals

"Setting goals is the first step in turning the invisible into the visible."

– TONY ROBBINS

SMART Goals

Are your goals SMART? Whether you are looking to change a specific aspect of your life or simply want to feel more confident or happier, goal setting is probably one of the most effective things you can do for yourself. You may already be seasoned at setting and achieving goals, or perhaps you prefer to just "go with the flow", but wherever you feel you are right now, having meaningful goals and plans for the future can greatly impact your present happiness.[78]

Goal setting with meaning and purpose can give you a clear sense of direction, keeping you focused and optimistic, with many positive mental health benefits to be had, such as feeling more in control and clearer in your decision-making. It can also encourage better mental health, physical health, and motivation, increasing your self-confidence and happiness.

In the final task in this book, you will use all the momentum you have built over the last four weeks to create a plan. You will choose what your plan looks like and how far in the future you would like to focus, but you may wish to consider some short-, medium-, and long-term goals to keep you moving forward. Use the insights from the exercises you completed (hopefully) earlier in week four, taking into account your purpose, what you want, and your "best possible self" vision.

Consider the categories: health and wellbeing, family and relationships, business or career, finances, and time freedom or life balance.

While having the right goals is important, taking action towards those goals is pretty imperative to their success, so the tool explored today uses the SMART framework with a positive psychology twist. Traditionally used in project management and business, the SMART tool offers a simple process to help build focus and motivation in many aspects of your life. Setting clear, actionable, meaningful goals, enables you to stay on track and connected to your positive outcome.[79]

SMART is a mnemonic acronym that was coined in 1981 by George T. Doran. While the letters have been adapted over the years and can have slightly different meanings for each individual, it is generally suggested that to ensure your goals are clear and reachable, and each one aims to be:[81]

- **Specific** (simple, sensible, or significant)
- **Measurable** (meaningful or motivating)
- **Achievable** (agreed, attainable, or actionable)
- **Relevant** (reasonable, realistic, or results-based)
- **Time-bound** (time-based, time-limited, or timely)

While this framework is really useful for diving deep into the details of what you want, there are a number of other tips that may make your goals easier (and quicker) to reach. Ask yourself these questions:

1. Why is it important for you to achieve these goals? Do you have a compelling reason to give this your full focus? Why does it matter? What will it give you (emotionally) to get this?

2. What are the consequences of not achieving your goals? What is the worst thing that can happen if you don't reach your goals? How might this affect you or those around you (emotionally)?

Connecting with your goals emotionally is key. It will be this emotional connection that will keep you focused and give you the strength to carry on when you really want to give up! Try also not to have more than two or three goals max at a time, ensuring that your goals are complementary and not conflicting with each other, as mentioned on day 25.

Some studies have demonstrated that writing goals down and sharing them with someone, instead of keeping them in your head, can increase your chances of achieving them by 33%.[82] You are also seven times more likely to achieve your goals with a support partner.[83] So, find a friend, work colleague, partner, or coach with whom you can share your plans for world (or self) domination and who can keep you accountable!

TASK 28

In your notebook, set yourself a simple, yet slightly challenging, personal goal that you would like to achieve in the next 3-6 months.

Use the SMART framework to guide you. Consider: what measures will you put in place, so you know you are on track along the way, and when will you know you have achieved your goal? What would success feel like? What one action can you take in the next 24 hours to get you from where you are now to where you want to be?

What will be the consequences of you not achieving this goal? How might you celebrate success? Who can you check in with to keep you accountable?

For a productive read, check out: The 12 Week Year *by Brian P. Moran and Michael Lennington* 🙂

Creating SMART Goals - Reflection

Did you find it in any way challenging to write down your goal for this exercise? Some common themes that occur when setting goals can include not knowing which goal to focus on (there are so many to choose from, right?) or, from a different perspective, not really wanting a goal. Maybe you know how you want to feel but want to be more free flowing. It also could be that you actually don't know what you want.

Some of the most interesting people I know don't yet know what they want, and the very thought of making that decision would cause them great anxiety! As this is a positive psychology book, the aim is to overcome and get rid of anxiety, so if goal setting feels too restrictive for you, maybe consider any feelings or values which you might like to focus on. In three months' time, how might you like to feel? Where might you like to be? Who would you like to spend time with? You can use the guide in the pdf workbook to help formulate your goals on: www.zeenahicks.com/28days-positivity

Next steps

You have two options:

1. Set long-term and short-term goals in each of the categories: health and wellbeing; family and/or relationships; business and/or vocation; time freedom; and finances. Create actionable steps that you will take each week towards achieving those goals.

2. Write a few observational notes on what you discovered, and enjoy living more positively!

Whatever you decide, it is your journey towards creating the life you want.

TAKE NOTE

WEEK FOUR - REFLECTIONS

Use this section to recap on the past week

What resonated with you the most this week?

Which exercise did you find most challenging in week four and why?

How can you close the gap between where you are and where you want to be?

Further Reflections:

FINAL WORD

A massive well done for reaching the end of this learning experience! While the book is complete, your journey of development and growth is only just beginning. If you have followed this book in order, you may now have more clarity on what you want, with a vision of where you plan to be in the near future and have started to form those first steps on how you might get there.

You are also equipped with an abundant toolkit of resources to continue to experiment with. Be brave with it, be bold, and be intentional every day. If you are hungry to learn more, or if there were any interventions or concepts that struck a chord with you, you can delve deeper into the topics by getting in touch with my team, reading the recommended book from that day or visiting some of the articles, websites, and research papers from the reference section.

Ending with the same question we started with: **Are you surviving or are you thriving?** Commit to owning your outcomes, by taking just one small action each day to be more positive than you were the day before. Most importantly, have fun on your creative journey towards positivity and living a happier, more fulfilled life.

REFERENCES

1. Peterson, C. (2008, May 16). What is positive psychology, and what is it not? Psychology Today. https://www.psychologytoday.com/us/blog/the-good-life/200805/what-is-positive-psychology-and-what-is-it-not

2. Klauser, H. A. (2001). Write it down make it happen: Knowing what you want and getting it. Simon and Schuster.

3. Craig, A. (2020, July 13). Discovery of 'thought worms' opens window to the mind. Queen's Gazette | Queen's University. https://www.queensu.ca/gazette/stories/discovery-thought-worms-opens-window-mind

4. Ruth, A. (2015). The health benefits of nose breathing. Nursing in General Practice, 40-42.

5. Zope, S. A., & Zope, R. A. (2013). Sudarshan kriya yoga: Breathing for health. International journal of yoga, 6(1), 4.

6. Porter, J. (2017). Why you should make time for self-reflection (even if you hate doing it). Harvard Business Review, 21.

7. Gotter. A. (2020). Box Breathing. https://www.healthline.com/health/box-breathing

8. Edelman, S. (2012). Change Your Thinking with CBT: Overcome stress, combat anxiety and improve your life. Random House.

9. Grimley, B. (2007). NLP coaching. Handbook of coaching psychology: A guide for practitioners, 193-210.

10. Peterson, C., & Seligman, M. (2004). Character strengths and virtues a handbook and classification. Oxford University Press.

11. Mayerson, N. et al., (2022) VIA Adult Survey. https://www.viacharacter.org/surveys/takesurvey

12. Niemiec, R. (2012). What Are Your Signature Strengths? https://www.viacharacter.org/topics/articles/what-are-your-signature-strengths

13.   Xiong, G. L., & Doraiswamy, P. M. (2009). Does meditation enhance cognition and brain plasticity?. Annals of the New York Academy of Sciences, 1172(1), 63-69.

14.   Van Vugt, M. K. (2015). Cognitive benefits of mindfulness meditation. Handbook of mindfulness: Theory, research, and practice, 190-207.

15.   Barbor, C. (2001). The science of meditation. Psychology Today, 34(3), 54.

16.   Mueller, P. A., & Oppenheimer, D. M. (2014). The pen is mightier than the keyboard: Advantages of longhand over laptop note taking. Psychological science, 25(6), 1159-1168.

17.   Ullrich, P. M., & Lutgendorf, S. K. (2002). Journaling about stressful events: Effects of cognitive processing and emotional expression. Annals of Behavioral Medicine, 24(3), 244-250.

18.   Adams, K. (2022). A Short Course in Journal Writing: It's Easy to W.R.I.T.E. , Centre for Journal Therapy. https://journaltherapy.com/lets-journal/a-short-course-in-journal-writing/

19.   Stone, M. (1998). Journaling with clients. Individual Psychology, 54(4), 535.

20.   Richter, M., Eck, J., Straube, T., Miltner, W. H., & Weiss, T. (2010). Do words hurt? Brain activation during the processing of pain-related words. Pain, 148(2), 198-205.

21.   Newberg, A. B., Robert, M. (2013). Words can change your brain : 12 conversation strategies to build trust, resolve conflict, and increase intimacy. Jefferson Faculty Books. 89.

22.   Emoto, M. (2011). The hidden messages in water. Simon and Schuster.

23.   Epton, T., Harris, P. R., Kane, R., van Koningsbruggen, G. M., & Sheeran, P. (2015). The impact of self-affirmation on health-behavior change: a meta-analysis. Health Psychology, 34(3), 187.

24. Allen, S. (2018). The science of gratitude. Conshohocken, PA: John Templeton Foundation.

25. Brozena, C. (2018). How Gratitude Can Reduce Burnout in Health Care. Greater Good Magazine. https://greatergood. berkeley.edu/article/item/how_gratitude_can_reduce_ burnout_in_health_care

26. Seligman, M. E. P., Steen, T. A., Park, N., & Peterson, C. (2005). Positive Psychology Progress: Empirical Validation of Interventions. American Psychologist, 60(5), 410-421.

27. Batat, W., Peter, P. C., Moscato, E. M., Castro, I. A., Chan, S., Chugani, S., & Muldrow, A. (2019). The experiential pleasure of food: A savoring journey to food wellbeing. Journal of Business Research, 100, 392-399.

28. Warren, J. M., Smith, N., & Ashwell, M. (2017). A structured literature review on the role of mindfulness, mindful eating and intuitive eating in changing eating behaviors: effectiveness and associated potential mechanisms. Nutrition research reviews, 30(2), 272-283.

29. Winnicott, D. W. (1991). Playing and reality. Psychology Press.

30. Savage, B. M., Lujan, H. L., Thipparthi, R. R., & DiCarlo, S. E. (2017). Humor, laughter, learning, and health! A brief review. Advances in physiology education.

31. Mora-Ripoll, R. (2011). Potential health benefits of simulated laughter: A narrative review of the literature and recommendations for future research. Complementary Therapies in Medicine, 19(3), 170-177.

32. Kataria, D. M. (2022). Laughter Yoga International - Health, Happiness and World Peace. https://www.laughteryoga.org/

33. University of Michigan Health System. (2008, May 6). Laugh Your Way To Wellness With Yoga Trend. Science Daily. www. sciencedaily.com/releases/2008/05/080505225405.htm

34. Fleming, M. (2005). Laffing Matters: A Grouch Prevention Handbook. iUniverse.

35. Sachs, M. E., Damasio, A., & Habibi, A. (2015). The pleasures of sad music: a systematic review. Frontiers in human neuroscience, 9, 404.

36. Pauwels, E. K., Volterrani, D., Mariani, G., & Kostkiewics, M. (2014). Mozart, music and medicine. Medical Principles and Practice, 23(5), 403-412.

37. Lord, T. R., & Garner, J. E. (1993). Effects of music on Alzheimer patients. Perceptual and motor skills, 76(2), 451-455.

38. Lee, M. M., & Park, B. J. (2020). Effects of forest healing program on depression, stress and cortisol changes of cancer patients. Journal of People, Plants, and Environment, 23(2), 245-254.

39. Joanne K. Garrett, Theodore J. Clitherow, Mathew P. White, Benedict W. Wheeler, Lora E. Fleming. Coastal proximity and mental health among urban adults in England: The moderating effect of household income. Health & Place, 2019; 102200

40. Kraus, M. W. (2017). Voice-only communication enhances empathic accuracy. American Psychologist, 72(7), 644.

41. Belin, P., Boehme, B., & McAleer, P. (2017). The sound of trustworthiness: Acoustic-based modulation of perceived voice personality. PloS one, 12(10), e0185651.

42. Smith, J. Y., (2022). Magic In You: How to rewire your brain. (2022). Lulu Inc.

43. Rogers, C. R., & Farson, R. E. (1957). Active listening. Chicago, IL.

44. Treasure, J. (2013). Conscious Listening. In Annual Meeting Proceedings. Million Dollar Round Table (pp. 93-103).

45. Burgoon, J. K., Berger, C. R., & Waldron, V. R. (2000). Mindfulness and interpersonal communication. Journal of Social Issues, 56(1), 105-127.

46. Chapman, S. G. (2012). The Five Keys to Mindful Communication: Using deep listening and mindful speech to strengthen relationships, heal conflicts, and accomplish your goals. Shambhala Publications.

47. Lancer, D. (2018, January 31). How secrets and lies destroy relationships. Psychology Today. https://www.psychologytoday.com/gb/blog/toxic-relationships/201801/how-secrets-and-lies-destroy-relationships

48. Gardner, M. R. (2017). Self inquiry. Routledge.

49. Van Baaren, R. B., Holland, R. W., Kawakami, K., & Van Knippenberg, A. (2004). Mimicry and prosocial behavior. Psychological science, 15(1)(71-71).

50. Newsom, J. T., Mahan, T. L., Rook, K. S., & Krause, N. (2008). Stable negative social exchanges and health. Health Psychology, 27(1), 78.

51. Harburg, E., Kaciroti, N., Gleiberman, L., Julius, M., & Schork, M. A. (2008). Marital pair anger-coping types may act as an entity to affect mortality: Preliminary findings from a prospective study (Tecumseh, Michigan, 1971–1988). Journal of Family Communication, 8(1), 44-61.

52. Carter, C. (2008, November 23). Conflict: It's a Good Thing. Mind & Body. Greater Good Magazine. https://greatergood.berkeley.edu/article/item/conflict_its_a_good_thing

53. Hilbrand, S., Coall, D. A., Gerstorf, D., & Hertwig, R. (2017). Caregiving within and beyond the family is associated with lower mortality for the caregiver: A prospective study. Evolution and Human Behavior, 38(3), 397-403.

54. Rowland, L., & Curry, O. S. (2019). A range of kindness activities boost happiness. The Journal of social psychology, 159(3), 340-343.

55.   BBC (2020, December 9). More than 900 cars 'pay-it forward' in random act of drive-through kindness. https://www.bbc.co.uk/news/world-us-canada-55254082

56.   The Random Acts of Kindness Foundation. (2022). Make Kindness the Norm. https://www.randomactsofkindness.org/

57.   Lyubomirsky, S., Dickerhoof, R., Boehm, J. K., & Sheldon, K. M. (2011). Becoming happier takes both a will and a proper way: an experimental longitudinal intervention to boost wellbeing. Emotion, 11(2), 391.

58.   Toepfer, S. M., Cichy, K., & Peters, P. (2012). Letters of gratitude: Further evidence for author benefits. Journal of Happiness Studies, 13(1), 187-201.

59.   Phillips, W. J., & Ferguson, S. J. (2013). Self-compassion: A resource for positive aging. Journals of Gerontology Series B: Psychological Sciences and Social Sciences, 68(4), 529-539.

60.   Dutton, J. E., Lilius, J. M., & Kanov, J. M. (2007). The transformative potential of compassion at work. Handbook of transformative cooperation: New designs and dynamics, 1, 107-126.

61.   Melwani, S., Mueller, J. S., & Overbeck, J. R. (2012). Looking down: the influence of contempt and compassion on emergent leadership categorizations. Journal of Applied Psychology, 97(6), 1171.

62.   Neff, K. D. (2011). Self-compassion, self-esteem, and well-being. Social and personality psychology compass, 5(1), 1-12

63.   Taylor, J. B. (2009). My Stroke of Insight. Hachette UK.

64.   Wood, A. M., Linley, P. A., Maltby, J., Baliousis, M., & Joseph, S. (2008). The authentic personality: A theoretical and empirical conceptualization and the development of the Authenticity Scale. Journal of counseling psychology, 55(3), 385.

65. Brown, B. (2010). The gifts of imperfection: Let go of who you think you're supposed to be and embrace who you are. Simon and Schuster.

66. Leider, R. (2015). The power of purpose: Find meaning, live longer, better. Berrett-Koehler Publishers.

67. King, L. A. (2001). The health benefits of writing about life goals. Personality and Social Psychology Bulletin, 27(7), 798-807.

68. Goodin, B. R., & Bulls, H. W. (2013). Optimism and the experience of pain: benefits of seeing the glass as half full. Current pain and headache reports, 17(5), 1-9.

69. Loveday, P. M., Lovell, G. P., & Jones, C. M. (2018). The best possible selves intervention: A review of the literature to evaluate efficacy and guide future research. Journal of Happiness Studies, 19(2), 607-628.

70. Vedantam, S. (Host). (2017, August 21) Decide Already. Hidden Brain. https://hiddenbrain.org/podcast/decide-already

71. Deci, E. L., & Ryan, R. M. (2012). Self-determination theory. In P. A. M. Van Lange, A. W. Kruglanski, & E. T. Higgins (Eds.), Handbook of theories of social psychology (pp. 416–436). Sage Publications Ltd.

72. Schwartz, B., & Schwartz, B. (2004, January). The Paradox of Choice: Why more is less. New York: Ecco.

73. Cuddy, A. (2015). Presence: Bringing your boldest self to your biggest challenges. Hachette UK.

74. Robbins, M. (2017). The 5 Second Rule: Transform your life, work, and confidence with everyday courage. Simon and Schuster.

75. Hirshkowitz, M., Whiton, K., Albert, S. M., Alessi, C., Bruni, O., DonCarlos, L., ... & Hillard, P. J. A. (2015). National Sleep Foundation's sleep time duration recommendations: methodology and results summary. Sleep Health, 1(1), 40-43.

76. Ferrando, S. (n.d). Benefits of Cold Shower: The cold cures. https://www.wellness.com/blog/13292441/benefits-of-cold-shower-the-cold-cures/simone-ferrando

77. Mooventhan, A., & Nivethitha, L. (2014). Scientific evidence-based effects of hydrotherapy on various systems of the body. North American journal of medical sciences, 6(5), 199.

78. King, V. (2016). Ten Keys to Happier Living – A practical handbook for happiness. Headline Hachette

79. Locke, E. A. & Latham, G. P. (1990). A theory of goal setting and task performance. Prentice-Hall, Inc.

80. Doran, G. T. (1981). There's a SMART way to write management's goals and objectives. Management review, 70(11), 35-36

81. Rubin, R. S. (2002). Will the real SMART goals please stand up. The Industrial-Organizational Psychologist, 39(4), 26-27.

82. Matthews, G. (2007). The impact of commitment, accountability, and written goals on goal achievement. Department of Psychology, Dominican University of California, Faculty Presentations. 3

83 Moran, B. P., & Lennington, M. (2013). The 12 Week Year: get more done in 12 weeks than others do in 12 months. John Wiley & Sons.

"The only person you are destined to become is the person you decide to be."

- Ralph Waldo Emerson

Ingram Content Group UK Ltd.
Milton Keynes UK
UKHW011821270323
419247UK00002B/3